Warrior • 111

The Hun

Scourge of God AD 375–565

Nic Fields • Illustrated by Christa Hook

First published in Great Britain in 2006 by Osprey Publishing,
Midland House, West Way, Botley, Oxford OX2 0PH, UK
443 Park Avenue South, New York, NY 10016, USA
E-mail: info@ospreypublishing.com

© 2006 Osprey Publishing Ltd.

A CIP catalogue record for this book is available from the British Library

ISBN-10: 1 84603 025 0
ISBN-13: 978 1 84603 025 3

Christa Hook has asserted her right under the Copyright, Designs and Patents
Act, 1988, to be identified as the Illustrator of this Work

Page layout by: Mark Holt
Typeset in Helvetica Neue and ITC New Baskerville
Index by Glyn Sutcliffe
Originated by PPS Grasmere, Leeds, UK
Printed in China through World Print Ltd.

06 07 08 09 10   10 9 8 7 6 5 4 3 2 1

FOR A CATALOGUE OF ALL BOOKS PUBLISHED BY OSPREY MILITARY AND
AVIATION PLEASE CONTACT:

NORTH AMERICA
Osprey Direct, c/o Random House Distribution Center, 400 Hahn Road,
Westminster, MD 21157
E-mail: info@ospreydirect.com

ALL OTHER REGIONS
Osprey Direct UK, P.O. Box 140 Wellingborough, Northants, NN8 2FA, UK
E-mail: info@ospreydirect.co.uk

www.ospreypublishing.com

Artist's note

Readers may care to note that the original paintings from
which the colour plates in this book were prepared are
available for private sale. All reproduction copyright
whatsoever is retained by the Publishers. All enquiries
should be addressed to:

Christa Hook
79 Lansdowne Way
Hailsham
East Sussex
BN27 1LT
UK

The Publishers regret that they can enter into no
correspondence upon this matter.

Abbreviations

Epit.	Vegetius, *Epitoma Rei Militaris*
ILS	H. Dessau, *Inscriptiones Latinae Selectae* (Berlin, 1892–1916)
Mul.	Vegetius, *Digesta Artis Mulomedicinae*

CONTENTS

THE HUN: SCOURGE OF GOD AD 375–565

INTRODUCTION

The Huns terrified people by their outlandish appearance, but it was their very name that soon came to symbolize the epitome of swift, merciless destruction. Branded by Bishop Isidore of Seville (d. AD 636) as the 'scourges of God's fury' (*Origines* 29), the Huns were Turkic nomads originating from the central Asian steppe. As hunters and herdsmen, they employed the horse and the bow for warlike as well as peaceful purposes. Steppe nomads had always been a threat to the settled agrarian societies, and around AD 370 the Huns began to migrate westward, launching a series of attacks upon the Germanic Goths, who in turn crossed the Danube and sought refuge in Thrace. It was inevitable that the Huns themselves would sooner or later cross the Danube, doing so for the first time in AD 395.

Ancient authorities

When the Huns first crossed into Europe they were illiterate. When they finally vanished in the turmoil of the 7th century, they were still illiterate. Apart from the archaeological evidence (bow and arrow assemblages, whitish bronze mirrors and cast bronze cauldrons) from the Danube region, we have to rely almost exclusively on what we are told by Graeco-Roman chroniclers for the story of the Huns. Owing to their perceptions of their impact upon the empire, contemporaries wrote of the Huns with fear and loathing, characterizing their culture as primitive and their behaviour as bestial. They were succeeded by Christian chroniclers, who condemned the Huns as devilish pagans and regarded them as an instrument sent by God to punish people for their sins. Civilizations are articulate, though the records are loaded against peoples who cannot answer back.

Ammianus Marcellinus (b. *c.* AD 330)

Ammianus was a pagan Greek from Antioch (Antakya) who saw active service under Iulianus II (Julian the Apostate) both in Gaul and on the ill-fated Persian campaign of AD 363, in which the emperor was killed. Written in Latin, the surviving

Attila the Hun, a medallion showing a demonic 16th-century portrait, Certosa di Pavia. According to Jordanes (35.182), Attila was snub-nosed, short, swarthy and broad-chested, with a massive head, small eyes and a thin, grey-sprinkled beard. (Esther Carré)

books of his *Res Gestae* deal with the years AD 353–78. His brief description of the Huns of his day is justly famous, even though he himself had never seen a Hun.

Publius Flavius Vegetius Renatus (*fl.* AD 385)
As a civil-servant-cum-military-theorist, Vegetius produced his *Epitoma Rei Militaris*, the dedicatee probably being Theodosius I (r. AD 379–95), arguing for a revival of traditional Roman military training and tactics. This work refers to the Hun bow, as well as to details regarding the adoption of the composite bow by the Romans. In his veterinary work on horse and cattle ailments, *Digesta Artis Mulomedicinae*, he describes Hun horses in some detail.

Claudius Claudianus (d. *c.* AD 404)
Claudian (Anglicized form) was a pagan Greek poet from Alexandria. Writing in Latin, he was the panegyrist of Flavius Stilicho and author of hexameter poems on imperial occasions and events, as well as of invectives against the eastern ministers Eutropius and Rufinus.

Olympiodoros of Egyptian Thebes (*fl.* AD 410)
His diplomatic career brought him into contact with the Huns, serving on an embassy sent out from Constantinople to the Hun king Donatus around AD 412. His history, which included a description of his mission and, apparently, a reasoned and erudite excursus on the Huns, has unfortunately been lost. From the surviving fragments of this work, it is clear that Olympiodoros' historiographical skills were considerable.

Priscus of Panium-Theodosiopolis (*fl.* AD 450)
Priscus was another visitor to the Huns, serving on the Roman mission of AD 449. He devoted a quite disproportionate amount of his book, *Byzantine History*, to a narrative of what he saw and did in the court of Attila. Writing for an elite audience, he was concerned with literary effect as much as accuracy. Even so, we are indebted to him for an unforgettable picture of Attila's timber-built palace, the etiquette of the royal repast, and an almost unbelievably detailed account of his own journeying in territories under Hun control, in which curiosity often extends to admiration. He published this work, eight volumes originally, of which only fragments remain, soon after AD 476.

Flavius Magnus Aurelius Cassiodorus (AD 490–583)
Roman scholar and adviser to Theodoric Amal, the Ostrogothic king of Italy, Cassiodorus wrote a Latin work entitled *De rebus Geticis*. Containing much information about the Huns, it is unfortunately lost to us. However, in AD 551 Cassiodorus did commission Jordanes, a Romanized Goth, to make a summary version of his work.

Zosimus (*fl.* AD 500)
Tentatively identified with the sophist of Ascalon (Ashkelon), the pagan Zosimus was the author of the Greek *New History*, up to AD 410. Though the valuable and first-hand account of Olympiodoros is lost to us, Zosimus used him as a source extensively.

Procopius of Caesarea Maritima (b. *c.* AD 500)

Procopius was a civil servant who served in a logistical capacity on the staff of Belisarius. Written in Greek, his *History of the Wars* is a contemporary account of the campaigns of Iustinianus' reign, including conflicts with the Persians, Vandals and Goths. Procopius' account ends with the decisive defeat of the Goths in Italy in AD 552, but a Constantinopolitan lawyer, Agathias, continues the story up to AD 558. His account is in turn continued by Menander Protector, a member of the *scholae palatinae* under Mauricius (r. AD 582–602), to Iustinianus' death (AD 565) and beyond (to AD 582).

Jordanes (d. AD 583)

Jordanes' *Getica* is a one-volume summary of the much fuller work (now lost) by Cassiodorus. It contains a character sketch of Attila (taken from Priscus) and an account of his invasion of Gaul. He also provides an account of Attila's death and burial.

Mauricius (r. AD 582–602)

The military handbook *Strategikon* is commonly attributed to this emperor. Its author basically codifies the military reforms of Mauricius, and most of the work is concerned with organization, equipment, tactics and operations. There is some duplication, but most of the advice is clear and practical. The penultimate chapter consists of four short essays giving strategic and operational recommendations for fighting Persians, Slavs, Huns and other 'Scythians'.

Anthony Quinn in the role of *Attila the Hun* (1954). Quinn tries his best with a diabolical script. Sweeping into Italy, Attila and his hordes reach the gates of Rome itself. Here they are stopped by the Cross and turned back by Pope Leo I. (Esther Carré)

CHRONOLOGY

AD

375   Huns cross the Tanais (Don).

376   Goths, fleeing Hun raids, cross the Danube.

378   Goths destroy eastern army at Hadrianopolis (Edirne); emperor Valens killed.

379   Theodosius I proclaimed emperor.

383   Army in Britannia proclaims Magnus Maximus emperor; he crosses to Gaul.

384   Flavius Stilicho marries Theodosius' niece and is promoted to *comes domesticorum* (Commander of the *domestici* protecting the emperor).

388   Theodosius defeats Magnus Maximus; Valentinianus II 'western emperor'.

389   *Magister peditum* (master of infantry) Arbogastes brings Frankish invaders in Gaul to heel.

392   Valentinianus dies; Arbogastes raises Eugenius as usurper in the west.

394   Theodosius defeats his rivals at River Frigidus (Wippach) in Pannonia. Arbogastes dies; Stilicho becomes western generalissimo.

395   Theodosius dies; empire divided between Arcadius (east) and Honorius (west).

396   Alaric, as *magister militum per Illyricum* (master of the soldiers of Illyricum), checks Stilicho's invasion of Greece.

398   Eutropius, chief palace eunuch, defeats Caucasian Huns invading Asia Minor.

399   Pannonia (Illyricum) returned to western jurisdiction; Alaric left 'unemployed'.

400   Alaric's followers declare him *rex Gothorum* (king of the Goths).

402   Stilicho checks Alaric's Gothic confederacy at Pollentia (Pollenzo) and Verona.
Stilicho recruits Alaric by making him *comes rei militaris* (count of military affairs) of Illyricum.

South face of the marble plinth supporting the Obelisk of Karnak, Hippodrome, Istanbul. Enthroned in the imperial box, Theodosius I, flanked by his nephew, Valentinianus II (right), and sons, Arcadius and Honorius (left), is receiving tribute from Goths, who kneel below. (Author's collection)

405	Stilicho checks Germanic migration led by Radagaesus at Faesulae (Fiesole).
406	Stilicho fails to stop Vandals, Suevi and Alans crossing the Rhine.
407	Army in Britannia proclaims Constantinus III emperor; he crosses into Gaul.
408	Arcadius dies; his infant son, Theodosius II, proclaimed eastern emperor.
	Stilicho falls to a palace coup and is executed.
	Danubian Huns under Uldis raid Thrace.
	Alaric seizes Rome.
409	Alaric raises the senator Priscus Attalus as puppet emperor.
	Alaric and Attalus besiege Honorius in Ravenna.
	Vandals, Suevi and Alans enter Iberia.
410	Alaric takes Rome and allows his men to pillage the city for three days.
	Alaric dies at Consentia, Bruttium.
411	Constantinus defeated at Arelate (Arles); Constantius becomes western generalissimo.
413	Theodosian walls of Constantinople built.
415	Constantius sends Visigoths to Iberia to fight Vandals.
417	Constantius marries Honorius' sister, Galla Placidia.
418	Constantius settles Visigoths in Aquitania Secunda (Aquitaine).
421	Constantius becomes co-emperor as Constantius III, but dies soon after.
422	Danubian Huns raid Thrace.
423	Honorius dies without issue.
425	Valentinianus III, son of Constantius, becomes western emperor; Galla Placidia becomes regent.
	Aëtius becomes *magister militum per Gallias* (master of soldiers for Gaul).
429	Vandals and Alans under Gaiseric cross from Iberia into Africa.
431	Gaiseric captures Hippo Regius.
432	Bonifatius is victorious at Ariminum (Rimini); Aëtius joins Huns.
434	Death of Rua; he is succeeded by his nephews, Bleda and Attila.
435	Treaty of Margus – Huns guaranteed trading rights.
437	Destruction of Burgundian kingdom by Aëtius and the Huns.
439	Gaiseric captures Carthage.
441	Huns cross Danube; Singidunum (Belgrade) and Sirmium (Mitrovica) razed.
443	Aëtius transplants surviving Burgundians to Sapaudia (Savoy).
445	Death of Bleda; Attila becomes sole ruler.
447	Hun invasion of Balkans brought off by Constantinople.
451	Hun invasion of Gaul checked by Aëtius at Châlons.
453	Death of Attila.
454	Murder of Aëtius.
	Ostrogoths settle in Pannonia.
455	Murder of Valentinianus.
	Gaiseric captures Rome and occupies it for 14 days.
456	Ricimer becomes western generalissimo.
472	Ricimer besieges Rome.
475	Orestes raises his son Romulus (Augustus) to purple (creates him emperor).
476	Romulus Augustus deposed by Odoacer; Odoacer becomes 'king of Italy'.
477	Gaiseric dies.
481	Theodoric the Amal proclaimed king of the Ostrogoths.
489	Theodoric defeats Odoacer at Sontius and Verona.
490	Odoacer defeats Theodoric at Faenza, but in turn is defeated at Adda.
493	Odoacer assassinated by Theodoric – Ostrogothic kingdom of Italy.
507	Franks under Clovis defeat Visigoths at Campus Vogladensis (Voulon).
524	Renewed war with Persia.
526	Death of Theodoric.
527	Accession of Iustinianus I.
528	Belisarius defeated at Minduos.
530	Belisarius' victory at Dara (Oǧuz) near Nisibis (Nusaybin).
531	Belisarius defeated at Callinicum (Raqqa) on the Euphrates.
	Khusro I proclaimed Great King of Persia.

532	'Perpetual Peace' with Khusro.
	Belisarius' *bucellarii* (retainers) crush Nika riots in Constantinople.
533	Belisarius invades Africa; Carthage retaken.
535	Belisarius invades Ostrogothic Italy.
536	Belisarius captures Rome.
537	Vitigis fails to retake Rome.
540	Ostrogoths surrender Ravenna and Vitigis to Belisarius.
	Belisarius recalled to Constantinople.
	Khusro captures Antioch.
541	Totila proclaimed king of the Ostrogoths.
	Khusro captures Petra; Belisarius restored to eastern command.
542	Khusro checked by Belisarius, who is recalled soon after.
544	Belisarius returns to Italy.
545	Totila captures Rome; Belisarius fails to relieve city.
546	Byzantines retake Rome.
548	Belisarius recalled from Italy and goes into retirement.
549	Totila recaptures Rome.
551	Kotrigur Huns ravage imperial territory; Utigur Huns are used against them.
552	Totila defeated and killed at Busta Gallorum (Taginae) by Narses, Iustinianus' general.
553	Narses defeats Ostrogoths at Vesuvius; Rome retaken.
554	Narses defeats Franks and Alamanni at River Casilinus (Volturno).
557	Truce with Persia.
558	Kotrigur Huns invade Balkan provinces.
559	Belisarius emerges from retirement and saves Constantinople from Kotrigurs.
562	'Fifty-Year Treaty' with Persia; empire pays tribute.
	Conspiracy to assassinate Iustinianus; imprisonment of Belisarius.
563	Belisarius reinstated at court.
564	Avars negotiate with Iustinianus to win concessions.
565	Deaths of Belisarius (March) and Iustinianus (November).

Szilagysomlyo treasure (Vienna, Kunsthistorisches Museum) from Transylvania, deposited around AD 400, containing 24 gold medallions depicting Constantius II, Valens and Gratianus, one with a barbarian addition of a frame of garnets. Other objects include cabochon gem-studded bow brooches. Probably a Roman gift to a local dynast. (Esther Carré)

HUN SOCIETY

'No human community is, or ever has been, entirely static: the society of the Huns was more dynamic than most.' Thus wrote the eminent Marxist historian of the 'barbarians' of this period, E.A. Thompson (1948: 3). The popular image of Huns rampaging across Roman Europe seems to be highly misleading. The Huns were not rough, uncultured herdsmen. They had been rubbing shoulders with agrarian societies for centuries, and had learned to value the qualities of these people and their culture while maintaining their own self-esteem. Hence by the early 5th century the Huns had adopted many cultural characteristics from those Germanic peoples whom they had conquered and from previous non-Turkic steppe nomads such as the Indo-Iranian Alans. They also became accustomed to wealth through booty and tribute and were able to buy the advantages of civilization.

European Huns, as opposed to those who had remained on the steppes, seemed to live a rapacious rather than nomadic way of life and

The Desana treasure (Torino, Musei Civici), which was found complete with trinket box, consists of costume jewellery clearly influenced by Roman traditions. The earliest artefacts date to the late 4th century and include these two brooches from the early 6th century. (Esther Carré)

should not be seen, therefore, as a purely pastoral society. One of our most important eyewitnesses, Priscus of Panium, found Attila living in a 'large village' (fr. 11) where the nobility had enclosures adorned with wooden walls, towers and even a Roman-style bathhouse. The available archaeological evidence from the middle and lower Danube region does not show a dramatic socio-economic change with the arrival of the Huns. It looks as if Hun villages, dominated by surface dwellings with wattle-and-daub walls and clay-coated floors, were plentiful on the Hungarian steppe (*pusztas*) and were well supplied with the fruits of agriculture and fixed settlements (Elton 1997: 26–29).

Before Attila

Their origin is, in truth, a mystery. Most often the Huns have been identified with the warlike people known as the Xïongnú (Hsiung-nü in Wade-Giles), a confederation of steppe tribes who harassed the Chinese at the end of the Warring States period (475–221 BC) and into the Han dynasty (206 BC–AD 220), but were eventually thrown back into central Asia. The major stretch of the Great Wall, in its various manifestations, was constructed on the Xïongnú frontier, and in the words of Sima Qian (b. *c.* 140 BC), China's earliest and most famous chronicler, 'inside are those who don the cap and girdle, outside are the barbarians' (Bichurin 1950: 1.38).

Yet a more effective form of resistance to these 'northern barbarians' may have been the adoption of some of their methods of mobile

Etrusco-Campanian bronze bowl (London, British Museum, GR.1855.8–16.1) for mixing wine and water, from Capua (*c.* 480 BC). The lid is decorated with four Amazons, two of which are executing the rearward 'Parthian shot', a technique that was emblematic of Asiatic horse-archers. (Esther Carré)

warfare. Against the protests of his nobles, Wuling of Zhao (r. 325–298 BC) changed into the battledress of the mounted tribes, carried out mounted archery exercises with his troops and then broke the hold of the nearby steppe tribes. Apparently, this was China's first unit of horse-archers (Selby 2003: 174).

Certainly the Xïongnú's devastating technique of warfare, terrifying to the Chinese, was precisely that used with such effect by the Huns some five centuries later against the equally civilized Romans – brilliant riding skills, combined with the use of a composite bow short enough to fire in any direction from horseback, even straight backwards over the animal's rump – the famous 'Parthian shot'. Too little is known about Hun origins to identify them positively with the Xïongnú, but the latter were decidedly Hun-like. Yet Han documents add to the problem by referring, at times, to anyone north or north-west of the border region as the Xïongnú: Xïongnú is a Chinese name, and the suffix 'nu', meaning slave, is a characteristically derogatory term for these 'horse-barbarians'.

Alternatively, the seeds of the Hun movement westward may lie in desperation. The nomadic tribes lived a predatory existence, keeping to their ancestral grasslands while the going was good, but prepared to invade the grazing lands of others and repel invasions of their own lands as severe weather conditions drove the nomads and their herds here and there over the central Asian steppe. Thus it may have been a series of particularly devastating droughts – a regular hazard on the semi-arid steppes – that broke the usual grazing cycles of nomads around the Aral and Caspian seas and spurred them on to new pastures, and thus to clash with the Alans and Goths.

Yet climate alone is not a sufficient explanation, for to a lesser tribe drought would have proved fatal. It seems likely, therefore, that the Huns were a confederation of Turkic tribes that moved westward. The nomadic way of life and the common hardships that such a lifestyle presented resulted in a degree of cultural unity among all the steppe-dwellers of central Asia. With the right mixture of need, self-interest and leadership, these ethnic nomad groupings could come together to forge alliances, and then would fall apart to fight among themselves with great speed. The nomadic peoples had a legend in which a mother figure rebuked her quarrelling sons by telling them each to take an arrow and break it – something they could do easily. Then she told them to put together as many arrows as there were sons and break them – something none of them could do (Selby 2003: 260).

Then again, this Hun movement may have been the result of a pressure of population. As it happened, the 4th and early 5th centuries in northern China were tumultuous, a time between the great days of Han and Tang, referred to as the Period of Disunion. The chaos lessened somewhat when a Turkic group, the Toba (T'o-pa in Wade-Giles), established north of the Yangtze a sinicized dynasty known as the Northern Wei in AD 386. Yet the emergence and collapse of dynasties may have sent shock waves of refugees westward. The rulers of northern China at this time, being of nomadic stock, certainly shared a cultural archery heritage with the Huns. They brought to China improved techniques in horse breeding, together with advances in saddlery and stirrups, which allowed further developments in mounted archery skills (Selby 2003: 187).

Cult of the sword

Many warrior-peoples worshipped, venerated or swore by their swords, sometimes seeing in one particular weapon a mystic symbol of divine support. The Scythians and Xïongnú both had their sword-cults. According to Herodotus, the Scythians 'set up an ancient iron sword, which serves as an idol representing Ares' (4.62.2), over which they poured the blood of prisoners-of-war. It is recorded that at the conclusion of a treaty of alliance between the Xïongnú and the Han dynasty:

> Chan, Myn, the *shan-yu* [chief of a tribal union] and the elders went up the Mountain of the Xïongnú by the east side of the river No-shui, and impaled a white horse. The *shan-yu* took a costly sword and moistened its tip with wine; they drank the dedicated wine from the skull of a Yue-chi lord who had been killed by the *shan-yu* Laoshan. (Bichurin 1950: 1.92)

The drinking of sacred wine from the skull of a detested foe thereby sealed the negotiations between the Chinese envoys and the *shan-yu*.

The Huns likewise had a sword-cult. Shortly after Attila came to power he made the cult his own. Priscus, later to be quoted by Jordanes, heard the original story. It seems that one particular sword – Latinized as the sword of Mars – had always been esteemed by the Huns, but had been lost. However, a herdsman noticed one day that one of his cattle was lame and that its foot had been cut. Following the trail of blood to its source, the herdsman found an ancient sword buried in the grass. He pulled it up and brought it to Attila, who 'rejoiced at this gift and being of great courage he decided he had been appointed to be the ruler of the whole world and that, thanks to the sword of Mars, he had been granted the power to win wars' (Jordanes 35.183 = Priscus fr. 10). It seems that Attila based his supremacy on the solid foundations of his people's ancient superstitions. Obviously anyone who questioned his right to rule would have to fight not only Attila, but the divine powers as well.

Under Attila

Attila (b. *c.* AD 406) at first ruled jointly (as the junior partner) with his elder brother Bleda until AD 445, when the latter died. No contemporary evidence exists to support the later allegations that Attila had had him murdered; however, the brothers were quite unlike and had always detested each other. Attila, however nefarious, had the attributes of greatness, whereas Bleda's principal occupation, so says Priscus, was laughing at his court buffoon, a grotesque Moorish dwarf called Zerko.

Image from a Greek children's book. Attila and his Huns bring fire and sword to the Balkan provinces. Though a very rugged and fragmented landscape, the broad plains of Thrace, of Thessaly and the south Danubian area were productive and relatively densely settled. (Author's collection)

The brothers were members of a dynasty that had united previously separated Hun groups around itself, together with many subject peoples (the majority Germanic) to create a substantial empire in central Europe, north of the Danube. Hun society was now much more sedentary, having established a capital near the middle reaches of the River Priscus named Tigas (possibly the Tisza, which dominates the central Hungarian *pusztas*).

Roman ambassadors, Priscus amongst their number, who tried to negotiate with Attila noted that even when gold was freely available the king himself still wore plain clothes, ate off wooden plates and never touched bread. The ambassadors found Attila sullen, capricious and arrogant, but as he was confronted with treachery on all sides this moodiness is hardly surprising. Attila's greatest crime was to be different, in physical appearance, cultural background and attitude towards urban civilization. It was his foes who raised him to the status of an alien monster. Thus his greatest memorial is his role as Etzel in the complex medieval German epic poem *Nibelungenlied*, which inspired Wagner's overblown operatic cycle, *Der Ring des Nibelungen*.

Under Attila's rule the Hun empire occupied an impressive area. In the north it extended to the Baltic, where, according to Priscus, Attila 'ruled the islands in the Ocean' (312.19). It did not quite stretch to the Rhine, for the Franks and Burgundians lay in between, but Attila was said by Priscus to rule 'all Scythia' (312.20), that is, all the lands west of the Caspian. Attila delighted in war, but after he had ascended the throne, his head rather than his arm had achieved the conquests

The Repulse of Attila the Hun (1511–14), Vatican papal suite. Leo I originally bore the features of Julius II, who commissioned the fresco. When Julius died, Raphael repainted the Leo I figure as Julius' successor Leo X, who had been one of Julius' attendants. So Leo X appears twice. (Esther Carré)

towards the north. During this period the Romans had successfully bought off their formidable neighbours, but now injudiciously allowed their payments of tribute to fall in arrears.

In AD 441 and 443, taking advantage of the fact that the Persians had recently launched an invasion of Roman Armenia, Attila invaded the Balkan provinces and defeated the depleted eastern armies with deplorable ease. In AD 447, favoured by recent earthquakes that devastated Asia Minor, he marched on Constantinople itself, the walls of which had suffered severe damage. According to Priscus (fr. 43) these massive land-walls, including no fewer than 57 towers, fell to the ground. Fortunately for the eastern empire, the fortifications were repaired and strengthened just before the arrival of the Huns. Attila turned aside and drove south into Greece and was only checked at Thermopylai. His next campaign was that of AD 451, when he turned west and invaded Gaul. However, he was defeated at Châlons by a western army under Flavius Aëtius.

Attila was far from curbed. In the spring of the following year he invaded Italy, sacking several northern towns, including Aquileia. By the summer, however, he was compelled to withdraw, short of Ariminum (Rimini), only by famine and its inseparable companion, pestilence. To spoil an illusion, when Pope Leo I (AD 440–61) persuaded the pagan Attila to turn back 'at the well-travelled ford of the Mincius' (Jordanes 42.223), he probably used such non-spiritual arguments as the height of Rome's walls, the current plague and the recent landing of an eastern army at Ravenna. He may even have paid a subsidy to Attila. Whatever

Attila's death by haemorrhaging during his wedding night was a dramatic ending to his adventurous life. In the 14th-century *Saxon Chronicle of the World* (Berlin, Staatsbiliothek, MS Germ. 129, folio 53) the dying Attila is portrayed not as a pagan marauder but as a Christian monarch. (Esther Carré)

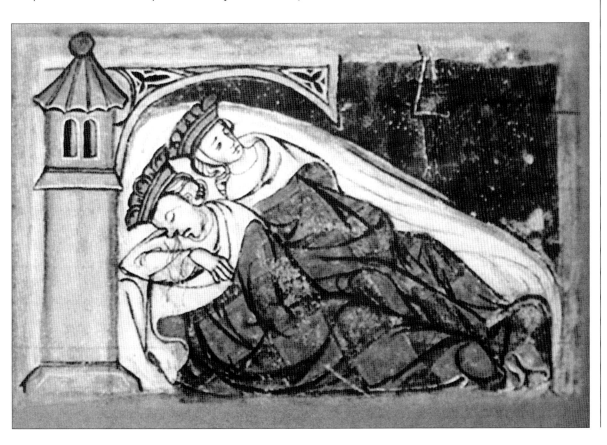

dissuaded him, however, Attila clearly intended to invade east again in AD 453. But within a year Attila was dead, dying unexpectedly during the night after his marriage to the Germanic princess Ildico (Priscus fr. 24).

Attila was a charismatic and powerful figure who demonstrated considerable ability as a super-tribal warlord. His successes, however, were limited. He could lay waste, with fire and sword, the Balkan provinces, but he could not penetrate further into the empire. His campaigns were thus pursued in support of a diplomatic policy whose main aim seems to have been the extraction of vast sums of gold as blackmail. In AD 443, for instance, when Roman armies had failed to stem his advance, Attila's terms had to be accepted – the immediate payment of 6,000 pounds of gold, and a future annual payment of 2,100 pounds of gold. In addition, every Roman prisoner who escaped from the Huns was to be ransomed at 12 *solidi* per head, and no fugitive from Attila's realm was in future to be received by the Romans (Priscus 282.26–283.3). His successes had been those of a plunderer, not a potentate.

Obviously Attila was not alone when it came to enriching oneself on the spoils of a troubled era. Many Huns saw the Roman Empire as a land of opportunity and were impressed by the ease of urban life, with its seemingly constant supply of luxuries and higher standard of living. They may have detested Rome as one will often hate a superior, but they also admired it and wanted to become part of a more advanced and wealthy Roman world, to enjoy its benefits themselves, preferably on their own terms. Procopius talks of the grievances of one Hun king, complaining that refugees from his rule in the empire 'will have the power to traffic in grain, and to get drunk in their wine stores, and to live on the fat of the land ... they will be able to go to the baths, and to wear gold ornaments, the villains, and will not go short of fine embroidered cloths' (*Wars* 8.19.16–17). Though a 6th-century report, this seems to be more representative of views held by Attila.

On Attila's death, his realm was divided between his sons. He had left behind him no true governmental machinery or institutions and, deprived of his forceful personality, the Hun empire soon fell to pieces. The subject Germanic peoples rebelled and defeated their overlords. The Huns broke up into their various tribes and never regained the unity that had made them a serious menace to the Roman Empire. The western and eastern courts alike were freed from the frightful threat that Attila had represented in his lifetime.

Engraving of the French stage actor Geoffroy (1804–95) in the role of Attila. Curiously, Geoffroy portrays Attila as a somewhat noble character, as opposed to one swollen with barbaric egotism. (Esther Carré)

After Attila

Ardaric, the king of the Gepids and former confidant of Attila, led a rebellion against Attila's sons, finally defeating them in AD 454 at the Nedao river in Pannonia (the exact location is unidentified). Attila's eldest son Ellak was killed. His surviving brothers, with the remnants of their followers, fled to the shores of the Black Sea. Meanwhile the eastern emperor, Marcianus (r. AD 450–57), recognized the Gepids as allies and granted Ardaric an annual tribute to the tune of 100 pounds of gold – one-twentieth of the ruinous sum his predecessor had paid Attila – and the former Danubian lands of the Huns (Jordanes 50.262–64).

Walls of Constantinople

In AD 413 the regent of the 13-year-old Theodosius II (r. AD 408–50), the praetorian prefect Anthemios, constructed new land-walls, a couple of kilometres or so west of those of Constantinus I. The new defences ran for 6.5 kilometres from the Sea of Marmara, taking in just north of it the Golden Gate (*Porta Aurea*), the triumphal arch erected by Theodosius I, to the Golden Horn. The Golden Gate, which owed its name to the plates of solid gold that covered it, was now to be one of ten gateways, five of which were used exclusively for military purposes.

The curtains were built of a double skin of limestone blocks, divided at intervals by brick-bonding courses five deep, with a core of rubble and concrete. They stood 10 metres high externally and 12 metres high internally, and tapered from 5 metres wide at the base to 4.5 metres at the apex. These were strengthened with forward-projecting towers, each 18 to 20 metres high and set at an average interval of 55 metres, of which 70 were square and 26 polygonal. Each tower consisted of an upper and lower chamber. The lower chambers opened straight into the city, but the upper ones could only be entered via the rampart-walk, which was reached by stairways located near the main gateways. Windows looked out from each tower-wall, while stairways led up to the battlemented roofs. Some 35 metres in front was a stone-lined ditch, some 20 metres wide and 7 metres deep with vertical sides, sections of which could be flooded to form a wet-moat if the city was threatened.

During the earthquakes of January AD 447 the land-walls were severely damaged, including 57 towers. Furthermore, Attila had just defeated the eastern army in battle and was now advancing on Constantinople, laying waste Macedonia and Thrace on his arrival. Meanwhile the praetorian prefect Flavius Constantinus, utilizing 16,000 Constantinopolitans under the direction of the Blue and Green circus factions, saw to the repairing of the defences. Within two months not only was this work completed, but also an outer wall (*proteichisma*), 8.5 metres high and some 2 metres thick, was built, complete with 96 towers. Alternating in position with those of the original wall, these new towers were either square or U-shaped and stood some 10–12 metres high. Between the main and outer walls now lay a 20-metre-wide terrace (*peribolos*), which not only provided a killing-ground between the main and outer walls but also served as an area for moving troops between these walls.

A bilingual inscription (*ILS* 823) on the south corbel of the outer gate of the *Yeni Mevlevihané Kapısı* (formerly the Gate of Rhegion) records, in verses, this extraordinary feat: 'In sixty days, by order of the sceptre-loving emperor, Konstantinos the Eparchos added wall to wall' (Greek); 'By command of Theodosius, in less than two months, Constantinus erected triumphantly, these strong walls. Scarcely could Pallas have built so quickly so strong a citadel' (Latin). A third couplet survives in the *Palatine Anthology* (9.690). Attila would have been confronted not by enticing gaps in a ruined wall, but by the whole restored and impregnable edifice.

With the collapse of Attila's empire, despite the chaos, the Huns did not degenerate into a band of brigands. After Attila many tribes obviously returned to nomadism, such as the Onogur (or Bulgar), the Utigur and the Kotrigur Huns, but continued to raid the eastern empire from the steppes of what is now the Ukraine. It was the latter tribe that posed the greatest threat, and Iustinianus I (r. AD 527–65) endeavoured to keep them from imperial lands, through various subsidies and treaties granted to them or to their neighbours.

Even so, in AD 551 a force of Kotrigurs crossed the eastern reaches of the Danube and plundered Roman territory. Strapped for manpower

Theodosian walls of Constantinople (Istanbul), looking north-west towards the triple line of defences between the Golden Gate (right) and the Second Military Gate (left). All the 11 towers that guard the main wall here are still standing, as are all but one of those in the outer wall. (Author's collection)

by this time, Iustinianus was unable to muster any of his own troops against them. Nevertheless, on this occasion he succeeded in diverting the Kotrigurs by inducing their neighbours, the Utigurs, to plunder their homeland and thus draw them back there. Since each tribe sought out its own pastures in comparative isolation, the tribal forces could act with complete independence from each other. Thus, as Iustinianus well knew, rivalry and hostility were as common among them as friendship and cooperation.

The Kotrigurs soon resumed their raids, and this time with a vengeance. Their chieftain, Zabergan, began a vast new expedition against the empire in late AD 558. He boldly divided his host into three bands, each with a definite sphere of operations: one assigned to Greece, one to western Thrace, and the third, under his personal command, to eastern Thrace against Constantinople itself. His audacity was justified by the circumstances of the Balkan provinces at this late period in Iustinianus' reign. The emperor's military resources were squandered or exhausted in his wars elsewhere. His treasury was drained by decades of expenditure. His fortifications were used mainly as places of refuge alone. The Kotrigurs ravaged at will, bringing fire and sword to the population of Greece and Thrace. Worst of all, they were soon pasturing their horses in the suburban gardens of the capital.

In this moment of humiliation and impending disaster, Iustinianus swallowed his pride and turned for help to a ghost of the past. Belisarius had been living in quiet retirement in Constantinople since his return from Italy in AD 548 (Agathias 5.14–15). Although he had long ceased active service, he had lost none of his energy or any of his astonishing tactical imagination. Quickly rallying to the emperor, he gathered what troops were available in the city. Most of them were worthless, though he had a core of some 300 men who were veterans of his campaigns, many of whom had remained with him as his personal body of retainers (*bucellarii*).

With these pitifully limited forces he marched out to defend the city and what was left of Thrace. Through a masterly use of ruses and skilful positioning, he tricked Zabergan's Huns into thinking they were about to fall prey to a great army. They abandoned their attack on Constantinople and withdrew from Thrace. Elsewhere the Kotrigurs' advance was finally stalled, and, laden with their booty, they straggled home. Iustinianus was in no position to strike the raiders on their way out of imperial territory, but he was able once again through diplomatic means to incite the Utigurs against the Kotrigurs (Agathias 5.25, Menander fr. 2). The two tribes thereafter wasted themselves in internecine conflict until the Avars, on becoming the new major power in the Danube basin, absorbed them.

As mercenaries

Other tribes, on the other hand, elected to settle inside Roman territory, garrisoning certain frontier areas as *foederati* (Barbarians) (Claudian *In Eutropium* 2.153), while others provided important sources of mercenaries for the armies of the western and eastern empires.

Ammianus (31.8.4) mentions in passing that among the horsemen that came to the dramatic rescue of the Goths penned in among the steep defiles of Mount Haemos in Thrace by a Roman army was a band

of Huns (autumn AD 377). It is not reported that this band had left the Goths before Hadrianopolis (summer AD 378). Immediately after the battle, when the Goths had a made a vain attempt to surprise Hadrianopolis itself, we hear of these same Huns again. Ammianus says that the Goth leader, Fritigern, 'had shrewdly won them to his side by the prospect of wonderful rewards' (31.16.3). There could have been no more than a few hundred, probably operating as outriders for the main Goth force, but they were the first Huns to reach Roman Europe.

Ammianus (31.2.2), Claudian (*In Rufinum* 1.325), Sidonius Apollinaris (*Carmina* 2.245) and Jordanes (24.127–28), when they first

East face of the marble plinth supporting the Obelisk of Karnak, Hippodrome, Istanbul. Goths of the *scholae palatinae* (household troops protecting the Roman/Byzantine emperor) protect Theodosius I (centre), Valentinianus II (right), and Arcadius and Honorius (left). As western emperor, Honorius would employ Huns as well as Goths. (Author's collection)

turn to describe the Huns, at once speak of their loathsome personal appearance. These writers can find no words strong enough to express their horror of the new barbarians, and Jerome (d. AD 419), scholar and future saint, neatly sums it up when he says, 'the Roman army is terrified by the sight of them' (*Epistulae* 60.17). The facial appearance and tattered skin garments of the new, horse-borne invaders may have unnerved the soldiers of the empire, but it is a well-known fact that the further removed in physical appearance, language and culture an ethnic group is, the more it is distrusted. And so the Graeco-Roman chroniclers saw the Huns as deceitful and fickle, hot tempered and greedy – savages of an exceedingly disagreeable kind. A typical description of the Huns runs as follows:

> You cannot make a truce with them, because they are quite unreliable and easily swayed by any breath of rumour that promises an advantage; like unreasoning beasts they are entirely at the mercy of the maddest impulses. They are totally ignorant of the distinction between right and wrong, their speech is shifty and obscure, and they are under no restraint from religion or superstition. Their greed for gold is prodigious, and they are so fickle and prone to anger that often in a single day they will quarrel with their allies without provocation, and then make it up again without anyone attempting to reconcile them (Ammianus 31.2.11).

Although he was an excellent authority, this particular piece appears to be an example of vilification on Ammianus' part. For the Huns are recorded as serving both western and eastern empires as faithful mercenaries on several occasions, and under Attila were assisted in battle by a variety of Germanic and Sarmatian allies, though it is true that after Attila's death a number of the Huns' allies turned on them and broke their power.

Hun mercenaries, for all their bad press, could be of considerable utility to a Roman ruler or commander. In addition to swelling the ranks of his army, a band of Hun horse-warriors, without links to the people, factions or particular regions of the empire, and loyal to their paymaster, could be a very useful coercive force.

In imperial service it is known that a Hun bodyguard had loyally served Flavius Stilicho (AD 365–408), the *magister peditum praesentalis* of Vandal descent for Honorius (Zosimus 5.11.4, 34.1, Orosius 7.38). Honorius himself maintained at least 300 Huns as part of his *scholae palatinae* at Ravenna (Zosimus 5.45.6), and in AD 409 he employed 10,000 Huns against Alaric (Olympiodoros *ap.* Zosimus 5.50.1). Olympiodoros, himself a first-hand observer of the Huns, underlines the extraordinary efforts that the imperial commissariat found necessary to make in order to procure the necessary supplies to support this force. Previously 'many Huns from Thrace serving under their native leaders' (Eunapius *ap.* Ioannes Antiochenus fr. 187) had fought for Honorius' father, Theodosius I, and we can reasonably assume that only Rome was in a position to concentrate a large force of Hun horse-warriors in one spot. Much later they would serve, albeit in much smaller bands, under Belisarius in Iustinianus' wars of grand reconquest. Procopius (*Wars* 3.11.11, 5.5.4, 8.26.13, 30.18, 31.3, cf. 7.12.10) writes of the Huns serving under their own chieftains for the duration of a campaign.

This was to fizzle out by AD 562 when a peace agreement between Constantinople and Persia, the 'Fifty-Year Treaty', was signed. The treaty contained very detailed provisions about frontier relations, including a clause that included the statement, 'the Persians should not admit either Huns or Alans or other barbarians to gain access to the Roman realm' (Menander fr. 6.1.317–18). Three years later the vision of a reunited empire died together with its instigator Iustinianus, and executor Belisarius.

The chief influence of the Huns upon Roman military thinking occurred after their demise. And so by the time of Belisarius' campaigns, nearly every cavalryman of the surviving half of the empire was armed with a composite bow, and most had gone one better than the Huns by having body armour and a heavy spear as well. Unlike earlier Roman horse-archers, these archer-lancers were capable of fighting hand-to-hand as well as skirmishing from afar. Moreover, Roman archery, based on the Hun model, seems to have been more effective than that of the Persians, or at least this is what Procopius (*Wars* 1.18.34) claims. The precise time of the changes is hard to pin down and it was probably a gradual process. Yet it is logical to attribute the impetus of these reforms

A Roman warlord and his retainers, 4th-century Great Hunt mosaic, Piazza Armerina, Sicily. Many of the most important figures in the empire, such as Stilicho, Aëtius and Belisarius, maintained retinues of armed supporters, most visibly in the form of the *bucellarii*. (Esther Carré)

to Flavius Aëtius, who had lived with the Huns as a hostage, commanded Hun mercenaries during the recovery of Gaul, defeated Attila and held absolute power in the west for over 20 years.

Bucellarii

Often 'outsiders' such as the Huns were excellent troops who provided reliable bodyguards for emperors and local magnates, as well as for generalissimos like Stilicho and Aëtius in the form of the *bucellarii* that surrounded them. In effect semi-private armies, *bucellarii* could be relied upon to follow their commanders wherever they went and, owing to the need for mobility, they were exclusively horse-warriors. The court-poet Claudian (*In Rufinum* 2.76–77) tells us that Arcadius' praetorian prefect Rufinus maintained an armed retinue of barbarians, and we learn from another source (*Chronica Minora* 1.650) that this corps was composed exclusively of Huns.

The term *bucellarius* – biscuit-eater – was derived from the word *bucellatum* – hardtack – and neatly reflects the fact that the commander himself supplied his *bucellarii* their daily rations. Liebeschuetz (1991: 45) makes the valid point that the men who joined these fighting retinues perhaps did so because their Roman paymaster could guarantee them

Dogmagnanc (formerly Cesena) treasure (London, British Museum) from Domagnano, early 6th century, containing an earring with garnets and pearls, a heavy gold ring, cloisonné necklace pendants, a large hairpin and a pair of mounts from dagger sheaths. The craftsmanship is Roman in origin, and probably belonged to either a Goth or a Hun. (Esther Carré)

long-term employment. According to Procopius (*Wars* 7.10.1–3), Belisarius travelled around the whole of Thrace and by offering money was able to enlist some 4,000 volunteers. For his African campaign Belisarius raised some 1,100 *bucellarii*, including 300 Huns, horse-warriors who had given a personal oath of allegiance to him (Procopius *Wars* 3.17.1, 3.19.24, 4.18.6, cf. 7.1.18–20, *Anecdota* 4.13).

One major consequence of waning imperial power was the emergence of provincial warlords who would control and defend areas against external pressures, both central and foreign. The practice of raising a semi-private army was technically illegal but on occasion it happened with imperial consent, especially in the west. Often such armies provided a lucrative source of trained men who could fight in overseas wars, but this development meant that emperors lost their monopoly of violence. Legislation was meant to restrict this behaviour, such as a law of AD 476 that made it illegal for individuals to maintain 'gangs of armed slaves, *bucellarii* or Isaurians'. But compromise was often easier, as it was a lot cheaper to uphold imperial authority in collaboration with such warlords, even if this effectively reduced the overall supremacy of an individual emperor.

As an institution the *bucellarii* are found during the barbarian invasions/migrations of the late 4th century, while the usage of the term was common by the 420s when Olympiodoros notes that 'in the days of Honorius, the name *bucellarius* was borne not only by Roman soldiers, but also by some Goths' (fr. 7.4). By the late 6th century, however, the *bucellarii* had been taken over and were henceforth paid for by the government and fully incorporated into the imperial army.

Organization and numbers

As the Huns came into contact with Roman Europe, nomadic hordes of untold numbers were claimed by 'doomsday' chroniclers – the classic example being Attila's army of 'half a million men' (Jordanes 35.182) – determined to make them seem overwhelming in order to excuse defeats or glorify victories.

Yet it is worth emphasizing that these pastoral people did not constitute immense, countless hordes; they rarely amounted to more than tens of thousands and their occupation of Roman territory usually involved little beyond the spreading of a thin veneer over the provincial populations in a given area. We should add at this juncture that we use the term 'barbarian' too loosely, for want of a better word, to describe non-Roman peoples who entered the empire. It is unsatisfactory because, as is the case with the Huns, it gives the impression that the battles and struggles of the 4th and 5th centuries were between the civilized Romans of the provinces and uncivilized intruders from outside the empire.

Hun economy was based not on agriculture but on all kinds of domesticated animals (Ammianus 31.2.3). Huns herded sheep and goats for milk, meat, wool and skins; cattle for milk, meat and hides; and riding horses to ease the problems of controlling large herds over vast distances. As nomadic herdsmen, accompanied by kith and kin, they moved around in small groups of extended families – presumably of the same clan, that most ancient of human socio-political units – continually seeking the best opportunities for grazing and trading as the seasons changed. Attila's Huns, for instance, included the Akatziri, subjects described by Priscus, who 'had many rulers by clans and families' (fr. 11). This arrangement was loose, and groups fluctuated in size as families moved from one group to another. Usually the number of families forming a group increased in summer and decreased in winter because of availability of pasture.

Each group, known as a herding camp, had its own hereditary pastures and probably numbered a few thousand. Driving their grazing herds before them, they trundled onwards, with their families and black felt-tents

Daughter of Theodosius I and sister of Honorius, Galla Placidia was destined to lead a remarkable life. Married twice, first to the Gothic king Athaulf and second (against her will, again) to the Roman patrician and general Constantius, co-emperor for just seven months. It was this marriage that catapulted her into power (Esther Carré)

packed in wagons, navigating the steppes like sailors on the sea (Ammianus 31.2.10). As a rule they followed set migratory routes and used traditional camping grounds for summer, winter and spring. Through this tough, if somewhat precarious, lifestyle they certainly learned from infancy how to endure cold, hunger and thirst: formidable attributes in any adversary (Ammianus 31.2.3–7).

On a plundering expedition a raiding force probably numbered about 1,000 horse-warriors at the most, with some grown men, alongside the women and children, left behind to look after the flocks and herds. Women would ride on horseback as much and as well as men, while their children, boys and girls alike, were taught from an early age to ride horses with and without saddles. In the time of Procopius, when the Huns had reverted to a form of social organization similar to that in which they were living in the late 4th century, their forces nearly always appear to number between 200 and 1,200 men, and Procopius says (*Wars* 8.3.10) that women were found fighting in their ranks. The expedition of Zabergan in AD 558, which aroused so much terror in Constantinople and was composed of 7,000 Kotrigur Huns, was a noted exception (Agathias 5.22).

We must not picture the Huns as wandering over the steppes in one enormous multitude – Hun 'hordes' is a misleading term. By looking at their methods of producing and appropriating food it is evident that a very large area of grazing land and hunting ground was necessary to support a comparatively small number of Huns. As they did not till the soil, Huns derived the bulk of their food from their herds and, much like other steppe-dwellers, they had to augment their supply by hunting and food gathering (Ammianus 31.2.3, Claudian *In Rufinum* 1.327, cf. Priscus *ap.* Jordanes 5.37). Additionally, Huns obtained their grain

Horde
By the 16th century the Mongol successors of Genghis Khan (d. 1227) were known in English as a 'horde', a term that has subsequently been applied to a very large number of animals or people, frequently on the move and often frightening or unpleasant. 'Horde' is the English spelling of a word from the Turkic group of languages, *ordū* – camp. Genghis Khan's grandson, Batu Khan, established the khanate of the Golden Horde at his camp in the area of Russia under his jurisdiction (1241) and the term gradually grew to encompass the whole Mongol military force, which amounted to virtually the entire nation.

Turkic felt tent (*ger*) with a collapsible frame, a latticework made of poplar and willow. Erected, the whole structure would be secured by stout pegged ropes. The felt covering provided good insulation and protection from severe steppe weather. The floor was covered with mats of felt. (Author's collection)

An important source of nutrition and household commodities, goats are light and mobile, and thus can cope with rough terrain as well as thrive on poor pastures. Heading for winter pastures, a Bulgar crosses over from Bulgaria into Greece with his goat-herd. (Author's collection)

through barter or as tribute from their settled neighbours on the steppe-rim. According to anthropological field studies conducted by ethnographers working among the nomads of Soviet Asia, a nomadic family of four required up to 260 kilograms of meat per year, 8–10 litres of milk or milk products every day, and 2–3 kilograms of grain or substitute. So every year 15–17 sheep (or 20–25 goats, or 2–3 bull-calves) had to be slaughtered for meat, and 4–5 milch cows or not fewer than 15 goats had to be kept (Vainshtein 1980: 104). To these we must add a string of horses for riding and a couple of oxen for haulage.

Skill

The nomadic lifestyle favoured those with physical prowess, who were quick with the bow and capable of outwitting the wiles of the hunted. And it was the hunt that served to hone military skills during peacetime when they were not needed to defend or expand the grazing territory. In his account of the Xiongnú, Sima Qian describes how the Han dynasty found itself faced with a new menace, that is, border tribes skilled in mounted archery:

> The Xiongnú had no written language: they governed themselves on the basis of the spoken word alone. Infants could ride a goat and draw a bow to shoot small birds and rats. As they grew up, they would shoot foxes and hares and these are what they used to eat. Their warriors were powerful archers, and all were armoured horsemen. Their custom when at peace was to follow their flocks, and thus archery and hunting formed part of their way of life. When war threatened, they practised battles and attacks so that

they could invade or make unexpected attacks. This was part of their very nature. (Bichurin 1950: 1.58)

Whether in the chase or on the battlefield, the bow represented the greatest empowerment of the individual, young and old alike, over his environment. As a youth, the Hun's challenge was to master the use of the horse and bow in battle and to persuade his elders by his courage in facing the wolf in the hunt so that he might, in time, make a worthy horse-warrior of a horse-warrior people. The Hun grew up in a society where there were no civilians. To be a poor fighter and hunter was to fail as a man and as a free Hun.

Individual nomadic households dressed their own skins and made their own clothing, footwear, felt, arrows, and so on. The softening of a sheepskin by two Scythians is shown here on a pectoral of Greek craftsmanship, 4th century BC, from the Solokha Kurgan, Ukraine. (Author's collection)

APPEARANCE, DRESS AND EQUIPMENT

The traditional and enduring image of the Huns is as savage 'horse-barbarians', distinguished not only by their brutal behaviour but also by their bestial appearance. This stereotyping of the Huns obviously originates with our Graeco-Roman chroniclers, to whom they were so unfamiliar as to be viewed with intense fear and horror.

Their chief refreshment was mare's milk, *koumiss*, which was drunk either fresh, as buttermilk, as whey, or as the intoxicating *kvasses*. Plain water was apparently abhorred. They ate all meats, producing their own mutton, goat, beef, game and horseflesh, which they either boiled in cauldrons or cured by drying them in the sun and wind without salt. Though the horse's primary role was as a means of transport, it also

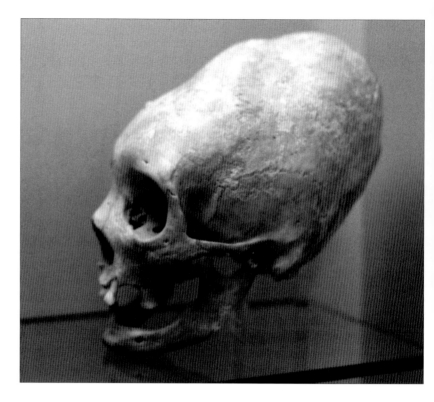

provided meat, milk, skin and hair. When they ran short of provisions on campaigns, they could survive on dried curds, wild game taken en route, mare's milk or even small amounts of their mount's blood. The horse was one of their most potent weapons, but eating horseflesh made them vile to the Graeco-Romans.

Appearance

Huns preferred to wear their hair cut back to the temples, leaving the part behind to hang untidily down to a great length, and shaved their cheeks, which were often ceremonially scarred as warrior adornment (Claudian *In Rufinum* 1.326, Procopius *Anecdota* 7.10, cf. *Wars* 1.3.4). As Jordanes writes, they cut their cheeks 'with deep wounds to mourn famous warriors not with womanly tears, but with male blood' (24.128, cf. 49.255). Huns also practised cranial deformation, making their skulls elongated, much like the Indo-Iranian Sarmatian nomads.

Quite a common practice throughout history, cranial deformation was created by binding in early childhood when the skull is still soft and growing. In some cases it was a sign that a child was destined for the priesthood, but in the case of the Huns we are left with a puzzle. Archaeology tells us that the Huns bound the heads of some of their children, who retained their deformed skulls as adults. Yet, oddly enough, no Graeco-Roman source records seeing any such thing. As the historian John Man suggests, maybe 'the long-heads were an elite' (2005: 66).

Dress

Huns, like other steppe nomads, wore a dress suitable for mounted herdsmen and warriors, what Procopius describes as 'loosely woven garments of a meagre nature' (*Anecdota* 7.14). Their short-sleeved tunics were made of natural wool or goat hair, worn to the knee and slit to the waist, where they were gathered by a belt. Breeches were worn loose and tied around the ankles. Tall leather boots would be standard, frequently of ox-hide and usually with heel-less, soft leather soles. Inside these would be worn felt stockings.

Voluminous kaftans were typically furred, with extra-long sleeves for use as hand warmers. Their design allowed flexibility for riding, as one breast crossed over the other and was tied, belted or buttoned to one side. For winter warmth two long fur coats were necessary, the one with hair turned outwards, the other with the hair turned inwards. Headgear was a goatskin cap, often with earflaps, or a felt hat trimmed with fox skin. Apparently, the type of fur worn indicated a man's rank: the commoner wore that of dog or wolf, a nobleman sable or squirrel. Garments were sewn together using a tough thread made of twisted sinew.

Equipment

As with all Asiatic nomads, the Huns' most potent weapon was the composite bow, in the use of which they were highly skilled. Yet light-spear and sword were also carried, as well as a lasso, a natural weapon for herders (Ammianus 31.2.9, Olympiodoros fr. 18, Sozomen 7.26.6, Malalas 364). Ammianus (31.2.9) speaks of iron swords, and these were generally of the long-hilted, long-bladed double-edged Sassanid type, designed mainly for cutting and thus suitable for mounted use. In addition to a sword, European Huns had a long dagger hung horizontally across the belly (Nicolle 1990: 14). The bow-case was usually carried on the front of the left thigh, whilst the quiver was hung either from a belt or across the small of the back with the barbs to the right.

For physical defence a small circular shield of osiers, wood or hide was carried, usually strapped to the left forearm (Maenchen-Helfen 1973: 253). Body armour of lamellar construction, reaching to the waist or knee, could also be worn depending on the social status of the warrior. Only a minority of Huns, chieftains and their retinues for instance, were normally armoured, but those who later served as mercenaries in Rome and Constantinople were expected to arm and armour themselves. Like their predecessors they doubtless acquired or purchased Roman or Goth equipment.

Probably originating in the Asiatic east, lamellar armour was made of narrow vertical plates (*lamellae*), which were laced together horizontally and vertically. Like scale armour, lamellar would have been a fairly inflexible form of body armour requiring additional *pteruges* at the vulnerable groin and armpits.

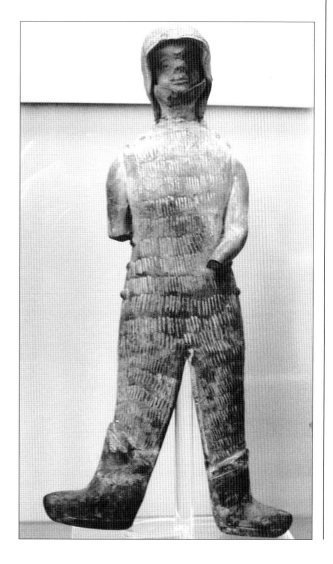

Painted ceramic tomb-figure (London, British Museum, OA.1936.10–12–24) of a Toba horseman, Northern Wei dynasty (AD 386–534). He wears lamellar armour with a hood covering his head. Of Asiatic origin, this type of armour was made of *lamellae*, which were laced together horizontally and vertically. (Esther Carré)

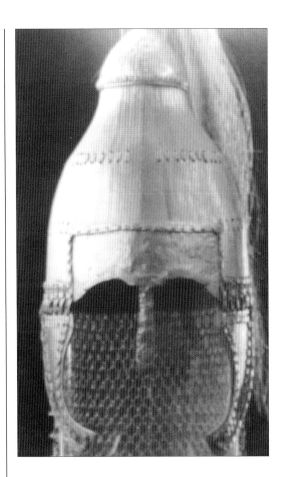

Procopius describes the injuries sustained by Bochas, a 'youthful Hun' who served Belisarius, as a spear thrust that penetrated him 'where his armour did not cover him, above the right armpit, very close to the shoulder' and another spear thrust that had 'struck him in front and pierced his left thigh, and cut his muscle there... He died three days later' (*Wars* 6.2.22–23, 32).

Iron *spangenhelm* helmets, usually acquired as booty, were also worn. These helmets, which probably originated amongst the Sarmatians of the Danube basin, were made up of several plates, usually six, held together in conical form by reinforcing bands. In their basic form they might be little more than a skullcap, but it was common to add cheek-pieces, neck-guards and nasal-guards.

COMPOSITE BOW

Composite bows of wood, horn and sinew, with stiffeners (ear- and grip-laths) of bone or horn, were the standard type of bow in the east and had been for millennia. Certainly clear representations of composite bows appear in Mesopotamia as early as the middle of the 3rd millennium BC. Despite its prehistoric origins, however, the composite bow was no simple stick and string. Technically it is one of the most complicated and most advanced artefacts among those made of perishable materials.

Alamanni *spangenhelm* (Stuttgart, Wurttembergisches Landesmuseum) from Grave 12, Niederstotzingen. This has an iron framework to which leaf-shaped iron plates are attached. There are cheek-pieces hinged to the frame, and a mail neck-guard. Hun horse-warriors usually acquired such prestige items through trading or raiding. (Esther Carré)

Form

Whereas self-bows are made exclusively of wood in one or more pieces, the composite bow has an elaborate network of sinew cables on its back, to provide the cast through resistance to stretching, and a belly of horn to provide the recovery of the bow through resistance to compression. The whole is built up on a wooden core. Stretched by stringing and stretched even more when the bow is drawn, the back is that side away from the archer and facing the target. Compressed by stringing and compressed even more by drawing, the belly is that side nearest the archer when he draws.

The design of the composite bow, therefore, takes full advantage of the mechanical properties of the animal matter used in its fabrication. Sinew has high tensile strength, approximately four times greater than bow wood, while horn has compressive strength. When released the horn belly acts like a coil, returning instantly to its original position. Sinew, on the other hand, naturally contracts after being stretched, which is exactly what happens to the convex back of the bow as it snaps back to resume its relaxed shape. Put simply, the sinew gives the bow its penetration, the horn its speed.

As the stave of a horn-wood-sinew bow is covered with strips of leather or bark and moisture-proof lacquers, it seems to the uninformed eye to be of one-piece construction. Yet, because it is technically a reflex bow, the distinguishing feature of it is the limbs sweeping backward from the grip when the bow is relaxed. Another distinguishing feature of many composite bows, especially those with their origins in the Asiatic type, is the notched ear-laths of bone or horn. These are rigid extensions of the bow limbs, set back at an angle from the limbs proper, which provide the weak ends with a rigidity that wood on its own cannot match. They also extend the length of the bow by a crucial few percentage points, and the extra length increases leverage. This allows the archer to bend a heavier bow with less effort, because each curving ear-lath acts as if it were part of a large-diameter wheel. As the archer draws the bow the ear-lath unrolls, in effect lengthening the bowstring. On release, the ear-lath rolls up again, effectively shortening the bowstring, increasing the acceleration of the arrow without the need for a longer arrow and a longer draw.

Fabrication

Steppe-dwellers had all the necessary elements – horn, wood, sinew and glue – to hand. Horn for the belly of the bow was likely to be from longhorn cattle. The horn needed to be soft enough to be worked

Scythicae arcus
The technical key to Hun success was the Hun bow, the best and most efficient to date and widely copied by other steppe-dwellers. The Huns also acted as a catalyst for tactical changes within the Roman army. Vegetius (*Epit.* 1.20) refers to *equitum arma*, probably the deadly bow of the Hun, and it seems that the Romans were only too glad to acquire these *Scythicae arcus* (Thompson 1948: 53). The bow certainly looked different because it was asymmetrical, that is, when strung its upper limb was longer than its lower limb (Nicolle 1990: 12, Karasulas 2004: 26). Oddly, asymmetry does nothing at all to the power, range, or accuracy of the bow. So its purpose remains controversial.

Yet Hun bows were also different in two other respects, adding up to a third that really did matter; they were bigger, at 1.4–1.6 metres in length; they had a more pronounced re-curve, which meant that greater latent energy could be stored in the bow; and, crucially, their size plus their shape gave them more power. Even so, being larger meant that the bow was not necessarily easier to handle on horseback.

Silver-gilt ritual vessel of Greek craftsmanship, 4th century BC, from the Chastiye Kurgan, Ukraine. A Scythian hands a strung composite bow to another warrior. A formidable weapon, it was the product of the animal tissues that support the steppe-dwellers' way of life. (Author's collection)

without splintering, but strong enough to withstand compression when the bow was drawn. That of a young animal was preferred, as it was straight and moist, and it was taken in the autumn when the horn was thick.

The wooden core was made of any non-resinous wood that took glue well. Maple seems to have been the core hardwood of choice, although yew, poplar and ash were sometimes used as well. The central part of the tree, known as heartwood, was preferable to the still-growing outer layers or sapwood. Cutting in winter ensured that the sap was down and the new annual growth ring had not yet started to form, and this had to be done along the grain of the wood. To increase the area of contact, the wood was deeply scored with a comb-like tool before the horn and sinew were attached to it.

When the horn belly had been applied to the wooden core, a backing of sinew was also applied. However, there is no way of knowing what species of animal they took the sinews from. The sinew lamination of more recent specimens was taken from the neck tendon of an ox, which provided long, narrow strips with sturdy ligaments. The longest sinews put the greatest tension into the bow, giving the greatest reflex and power. The gluing of horn to wood was usually carried out in the winter when cooler, humid conditions slowed and thus toughened the setting. Sinew was better applied on a warm spring day.

Fish glue was probably used, as it is the most dynamic of the collagen-based glues, though tendon glue, made from boiled tendons, could serve as a viable alternative. Glue of lesser quality was made from boiled hides. Such water-soluble glues readily absorbed moisture, rendering bows useless in relative humidity above 70 per cent. The glue could take up to a year to fully cure. As the glue and sinew dried they shrank, which pre-tensioned the bow and made it re-flex; that is, the curvature unstrung was opposite to the curvature when strung.

Replicas

A completed composite bow was a *tour de force* of precision engineering and bonding. Modern replicas start with a belly made of two pieces of horn spliced at the centre of the grip, or one piece of longhorn the full length. A hardwood core is then glued to the horn belly. The ear-laths are then V-spliced and attached to the core with glue. Layers of sinew are then applied to the core and around the joint of the horn and limb, followed, after tillering, by a layer of leather or birch bark to render the bow waterproof. Finally, bone plates are applied to the sides of the ear-laths and grip.

Birch bark was a favourite waterproofing material (particularly when peeled from young trees) and would be boiled for two or three days to retain its pliability. Similarly, horn is boiled so as to soften and flatten it, after which both sides are shaved so that they are flat and parallel. The core wood is prepared by making it into parallel strips, leaving one end unfinished for the splice and joint. A V-splice is cut into the end of this core lamination for the top and bottom ear-laths. These are shaped into long rectangular pieces that are oversized enough to allow a V-splice and joint. The joint for the V-splice is achieved by cutting a diamond-shaped piece of hardwood that will attach the horn to the core lamination at the required angle.

The horse warrior

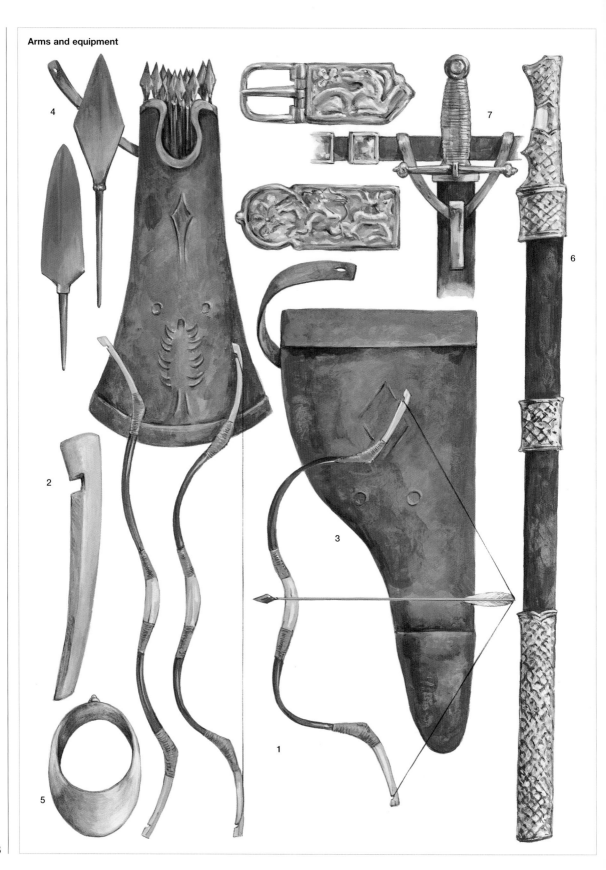

Arms and equipment

B

The Parthian shot

Battle of Châlons

E

Spoils of war

F

The core, splice and horn are glued together and shaped to the finished size. Once set, a grip-lath is glued onto the backside of the bow and then the sinew is added. The latter will add much of the draw weight, six to eight layers being the norm. Once the sinew is dry, tillering can be achieved by scraping the horn carefully.

Bowstrings

Naturally, to draw a bow there must be a string between both ends. The bowstring needs to be of a material that does not stretch too easily, and must be neither too heavy nor too light for the bow. As the string is constantly under a lot of stress, and must not stretch or break, bowstring technology is just as important as the bow itself. Bowstrings were commonly made of twisted gut or sinew, horsehair, and perhaps matter such as certain vines, and sometimes silk. Archers always carried spares, partly for use in different climatic conditions. Horsehair strings, for example, are best suited to cold climates, unlike sinew strings, which absorb moisture and stretch.

An important characteristic of the composite bow, which suited it for warfare, was that it could be kept strung for long periods of time without losing power like a wooden self-bow. In fact composite bows function better when kept under tension, and the ready-strung bow in its case certainly made quick firing possible, the weapon being pretty well 'loaded' and ready for use.

Arrows

A bow relies on sending an arrow deep into the body of its victim. As the arrow passes through it severs blood vessels and major arteries. Since arrows ordinarily kill by bleeding, projectiles that can open up a large wound are advantageous. Because human ribs are horizontal and the bow held vertically, the head of a war arrow is often perpendicular to the plane of the notch, so that the point may pass more easily between the ribs. For the same reason, the plane of the head matches that of the notch in hunting arrows. The other major difference between a hunting arrowhead and a war arrowhead is one of dimension. The former has narrow shoulders so it can be withdrawn from the carcass and used again, but the blade of an arrow used against man is short and broad, with hooked shoulders, making it difficult to extract.

Arrowheads were mainly of the tang type, although the socket type was employed as well. Experimental archaeology has shown that the latter type tended to break behind the socket itself. Whether this breaking action was deliberately intended, or simply occurred as an accidental by-product of manufacture, is hard to ascertain. According to the physician Paulus Aegineta (6.88.2), this was done with the intention of complicating the extraction. As Homer says 'a healer is worth an army full of other men at cutting shafts out, dressing arrow wounds' (*Iliad* 11.514–15). Yet according to the soldier Ammianus (31.15.11), the purpose was to prevent the enemy from reusing its own arrows. These two passages are salutary reminders of how an author's intellectual background and the contents and the aims of his work can influence his view of things.

Though tanged arrowheads proved less likely to break on impact, the sinew binding required to hold the point in place limited their degree of

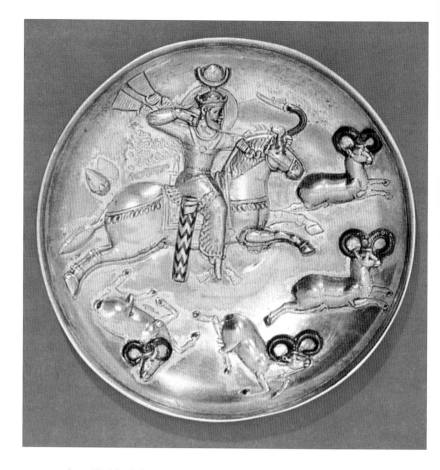

penetration. Field trials were conducted against all known forms of Roman armour. Not surprisingly, mail (*lorica hamata*) proved to be the easiest to penetrate, followed by scale (*lorica squamata*) and finally segmented (*lorica segmentata*), in which none of the arrowheads penetrated to a depth sufficient to cause a fatal wound even at a range of 7 metres. Somewhat surprisingly the wooden shield, especially if covered with leather, provided almost as much defence (Massey 1994: 36–39).

Shafts were made from wood (birch, hornbeam, ash, cornel, rose-willow), cane or reed. Where cane or reed was used, the arrowhead was first attached to a wooden pile, which was then glued and bound on to the shaft. The piles reduced the risk of the cane or reed splitting on impact, which would, if it occurred, reduce the arrow's penetrative power.

While arrows of wood and cane are less likely to break, reed is one of the best materials, having a combination of lightness, rigidity and elasticity ideal for shafts. Reeds are also already well adapted to their aerodynamic role as shafts by their need, while growing, to maintain an evenly round profile to reduce wind drag, as well as by having the elasticity and strength to bend and return to an upright position. This latter adaptation is critical. An arrow needs to be able to bend round the bow when released, and flex so that its tail swings clear of the bow before resuming the path along which it was aimed at the moment of release (the so-called archer's paradox). Also, reed shafts can quickly absorb the vibration of being loosened and thus straighten out more quickly than wooden ones.

Release

The art of archery has noticeable stylistic variations, and five distinct methods of releasing an arrow are practised. In the primary method the straightened thumb and the first and second joints of the bent forefinger grasp the butt end of the arrow. Pulling on the arrow pulls the bowstring back. The secondary release is a development of the primary release. Only the thumb and forefinger grasp the arrow, with the second, third and fourth fingers on the bowstring assisting the draw. The third type is very similar, but recognized as a separate technique. The arrow is again grasped between thumb and forefinger, but here the forefinger is also on the string to assist the drawing of the bow. None of the above methods require the arrow to be sufficiently notched to fit on the bowstring.

In the Mediterranean and Mongolian (or Chinese) styles only the bowstring is drawn. With the first technique the bowstring is drawn back to the chin or chest by the tips of three fingers with the arrow lightly held like a cigarette, if held at all, between the first and second fingers. The fourth finger and thumb are not used. A later variation of this technique is the Flemish release. This only employs the first and second fingers, one above the arrow and the other below it, and is very efficient if the fingers are strong enough to stand the strain. Apparently, it was this particular method that gave rise to the infamous 'Up Yours!' two-fingered salute. With the back of the hand facing the viewer, the hand is raised, in anger or tauntingly, sometimes fast and sometimes slow, towards the sky. It is said that the French at Agincourt (25 October 1415) swore to mutilate any captured archer by severing his drawing fingers and, in return, after the battle the English bowmen reciprocated by gesturing that they still had the necessary digits as if to say to the French 'Here's my two fingers – come and get them, if you can.'

The Mongolian release, on the other hand, employs the thumb only, the strongest single digit, with a thumb-ring of bone or horn worn as protection from bowstring pressure and friction. This allows the pressure to be brought on the bowstring at a single point close to the arrow nock, rather than spreading the pressure over a greater surface as occurs with the three fingers of the Mediterranean release.

The thumb-ring is placed on the thumb of the draw-hand, with the bowstring lying in a slight depression in the ring's surface. The hole is oval and not circular, the purpose being to ensure that the ring sits snugly on the thumb. The expert archer puts the ring near the base of his thumb. The forefinger clenches the thumb inwards, with the remaining fingers curled into a fist. Assuming the archer draws with his right hand, the arrow is placed on the right-hand side of the bow grip, opposite to that met with any other form of release. When the archer nocks the arrow and pulls the bowstring, the ring slides gradually forward to arrive at the fold of the thumb-joint.

The thumb-draw is a faster draw, allowing greater speed of delivery, and it also helps prevent the bowstring bruising the left forearm, which can disrupt the aim. Moreover, it is physically more awkward to draw back a bowstring beyond the centre of the body with the fingers hooked over the string, but with a thumb-ring it becomes easier. However, the method is far more difficult to master than any other method, and it requires endless practice for an archer to

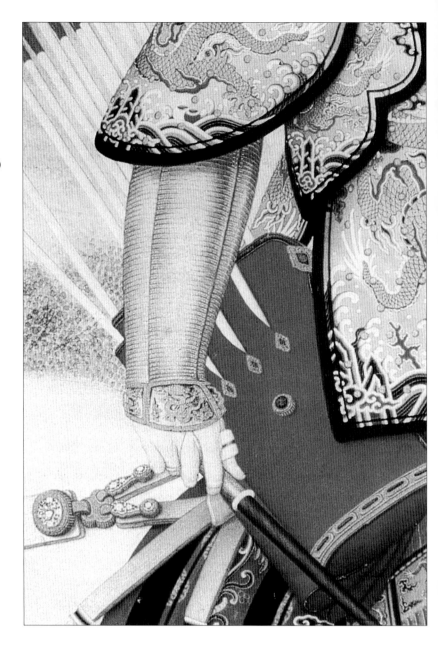

become proficient in this technique. If, for example, the ring is put on the fold of the thumb-joint itself, the archer cannot apply proper force when he draws and it is easy to slip and misfire. In all probability, although the Mongolian style is better for shooting on horseback, the method of release would have revolved around either individual or tribal preference.

Ancillary equipment

Archers using the Mediterranean release required the use of a leather bracer on the left forearm, the bow being held in the left hand, to protect it from the backlash of the bowstring. Leather 'shooting tabs' to protect the archer's fingers from the bowstring may also have been employed. Whilst a bracer was not required for the Mongolian release, a thumb-ring was needed so as to draw and hold the bowstring without cutting the thumb.

The bow required a case and the arrows a quiver, both of which must be large enough to completely encase their respective contents, as both bow and arrows were sensitive to damp conditions. The strung bow was kept in a broad case, usually hung on the left with the quiver on the right. The Huns used two patterns of quiver, one being tube-like and the other hour-glass shaped with a closing flap. The shape of the latter was designed to accommodate the fletching of arrows carried point up for easier arrowhead selection. Cases and quivers were made of perishable materials, such as leather, bark or wood, and few remains survive other than pictorial representations.

Performance

Combining layers of sinew, wood and horn creates a bow with a balance of strength under tensile and compressive forces, so facilitating an efficient transfer of the potential energy stored in the draw to the arrow. As little or no energy is dissipated in the kick and oscillation that characterize other bows, a composite bow imparts a greater degree of force to the arrow when fired. Unlike a wooden self-bow of the same draw weight, the more powerful composite bow offers the archer a choice of two tactical options. Either he can deliver a lightweight projectile over a distance twice that which a self-bow can shoot, or he can deliver a projectile of greater weight at short range when the capacity to pierce armour or to thoroughly disable an opponent is needed (McEwen 1978: 189).

The actual range and performance of the composite bow are open to debate, and a number of varied figures have been suggested. Vegetius (*Epit.* 2.23) recommended a practice range of 600 Roman feet (*c.* 580ft, 177m), while later Islamic works expected an archer to display consistent accuracy at 69 metres. Modern research tends to place an accurate, flat trajectory range up to 50–60 metres, with an effective range extended at least 160–175 metres, and a maximum range at between 350 and 450 metres (McLeod 1965: 8).

Range and performance are also dependent upon bow quality. The better the weapon is made, and the better it is tailored to an individual archer's height and strength, the better the performance. Yet range is as much reliant upon the man as the bow. Unlike firearms or weapons such as the crossbow, which store chemical or potential energy and, by releasing this, propel their missile, a bow converts the bodily strength of the firer into the force propelling the arrow.

Other external factors to consider are those of accuracy and effectiveness. Though the target's size and rate of movement, as well as the skill of the individual archer, governed accuracy, in actuality the archer would have practised shooting at a stationary target. The accuracy with which the Huns used their bows never failed to astonish Graeco-Roman observers (Ammianus 31.2.9, Olympiodoros fr. 19, Sidonius *Carmina* 2.266–69, Procopius *Wars* 1.21.27, Jordanes 24.128, cf. 48.249, 49.255). However, whilst this level of accuracy – the ability to pick off individuals – would have been useful in the archer's role as a skirmisher (Herodian 6.7.8, 7.2.2), the archer's main task was to shoot, indirectly, at a large enemy troop formation.

Firing technique

Steppe horse-archers used the technique of firing at a fairly high elevation, perhaps as much as 45 degrees, so that arrows fell almost vertically on to the enemy. In this case accuracy was more concerned with all of the arrows arriving on the target area at the same time than with individual marksmanship. Effectively, the firer was shooting at a unit rather than an individual. In this case, an effective shot is not necessarily an accurate one, and in pitched battle a murderous barrage is possible even without aiming. The second factor, effectiveness, was itself governed by two factors, namely the target's vulnerability and the type of arrowhead used. Ammianus says that the Huns used arrows tipped with sharpened bone 'as hard and murderous as iron' (31.2.9). But none have survived that can be assigned to the Huns, and such arrowheads, if used, were quickly replaced by iron when this became readily available through trading or raiding.

It is not just a question of being an accurate shot that makes a good archer – there are other equally important matters, particularly on the field of battle. The devastation caused by arrows was considerable, but no less effective was the psychological impact. The literary sources frequently speak of the fear that an arrow storm could provoke in an enemy. There is a logical reason for this particular phenomenon. Whereas soldiers in battle can brace themselves to an advance of infantry with sword and spear – a positive danger that can be readily observed, anticipated and suitably countered – the unexpected poses less of a positive threat and is therefore more difficult to combat. The suddenness of massed arrows raining down from who knows where must have been terrifying, particularly if each barrage consisted of hundreds, if not thousands, of arrows in one hissing and thudding cloud.

The mounted archer and his horse operated as virtually one being. When firing the bow from horseback, a combination of movements – the forward motion and bounce of the gallop, the shock of hooves and flailing arms – and any roughness of terrain considerably disrupt the aim. It is necessary, therefore, for the horse-archer to loose his arrow only when the horse is in flight; that is, a split-second opportunity when all legs in full gallop are off the ground. With a lifetime's experience, aiming is done instinctively, all the time allowing for the specific characteristics of the bow, variables such as wind, distance and target, and the horse's movements. The horse-archer has to be not only a sure shot, but also a superb horseman. When shooting from horseback both hands are used in firing, leaving control of the horse to leg pressure alone. Riding hands-free was a practised skill needed in herding and hunting. The horse, needless to say, must be reliable.

Yet for the horse-archer a major stumbling block was the need to fire one arrow after another at speed. For speed of reloading and drawing, the bow relied on the arrows being in the hand rather than in the archer's quiver. According to Li Chengfen, who at the very end of the Ming dynasty (1368–1644) wrote his little-known *Archery Manual*, it is a hopelessly slow process to reload the bow by reaching down to your waist or over your shoulder:

> When it comes to target archery on horseback, there are some who stick arrows into their collars or belts; neither is effective. For

Electrum ritual vessel of Greek craftsmanship, 4th century BC, from the Kul-Oba Kurgan, Crimea. A Scythian strings his composite bow by bracing it behind his knee. Great force is required, and when strung the weapon has enormous tension. (Author's collection)

effectiveness, you should always take two arrows, grasping one firmly against the grip of the bow while nocking the other on the string. (Quoted in Selby 2003: 303)

The revival of the long-vanished skill of mounted archery by the Hungarian Lajos Kassai has, amongst myriad other details, single-handedly revealed beyond mere words how to fire quickly from the back of a galloping horse. First forget the quiver, as this is merely to store those arrows not about to be fired. In the words of John Man (2005: 90):

This is how it is done: hold a bunch of arrows in the left hand against the bow, making sure they are spread like an array of cards; reach between string and bow; grip an arrow with two fingers bent double so that they form firm supports either side; place thumb just so; pull the arrow back so that the string slides along the thumb straight into the nock in the arrow; and pull, while raising the bow, all in one smooth set of actions.

Kassai, the acknowledged master of mounted archery, can fire three arrows in six seconds, a shot every two seconds.

HORSES

It was the horse that gave the central Asian nomad his amazing military power. The advantages to a warrior of being mounted are various. Apart from the obvious vast improvements in mobility, there is also the advantage of an elevated position from which to fight earthbound opponents. Likewise, there are the physical and psychological effects of the relatively large and powerful animals themselves. Raised upon the grasslands in enormous numbers, these animals were not, however, in inexhaustible supply. Horses, bows and speed of manoeuvre, rather than numbers, made the steppe nomad virtually invincible within his own domain.

Type

The horses the Huns rode were tough, rough-coated mounts with short legs, common to the steppes. Although only 12–14 hands high, they

Seventh-century *Hanswa* horse (Edinburgh, Royal Museum, 10.73–76). The incised line terminating in a loop represents a simple, mounting stirrup. Attached to only one side of the saddle, this stirrup provided the rider with an easier and safer method of mounting his horse. (Author's collection)

were muscular and had great stamina. Their smallness gave the Huns considerable control over them and thus provided a stable platform for archery as well as hand-to-hand fighting. Many of the stallions were gelded to make them easier to handle. This custom had ancient origins: from findings in Pazyryk burials, it would appear that noblemen rode only geldings (Rudenko 1970: 118), and the fact that the Scythians practiced castration is mentioned by Strabo (7.4.8). The Huns preferred whites, greys, blacks and chestnut colours, the lightest hues being reserved for warriors of rank. The animals were marked either by branding with the clan emblem (*tamga*), a simple design, or by cutting a pattern (*im*) on the ears, an ancient custom among the steppe nomads (Maenchen-Helfen 1973: 210, Vainshtein 1980: 101–03).

Steppe breeds in general can feed on virtually any quality of pasturage, fending for themselves in the very severe conditions of the steppes, where even in summer a typical day may be a chilly 12 degrees centigrade and windy. Coping well and gaining sustenance in a particularly harsh environment would give critical advantage to horse-warriors on extended raids, as their mounts would not require the carting of fodder but were simply let loose at the end of a day's riding to fend for themselves. Such horses were a serious advantage for anyone intent on quick raiding over any distance at any time of the year. The Huns thus had a horse that was not only universally resilient, but also low maintenance, and these qualities were not lost on the Romans, even if the horses were contemptuously referred to as 'hardy but ugly beasts' (Ammianus 31.2.5).

It is Vegetius who describes for us the Hun horse in some detail; indeed it is even given pride of place by the author:

> Hun horses have large heads curved like hooks, protruding eyes, narrow nostrils, broad jaws, strong and rigid necks. Their manes hang down to their knees, their ribs are big, their backbones curved, and their tails shaggy. They have very strong shinbones and small feet, their hooves being full and broad, and their soft parts hollow. Their whole body is angular with no fat at all on the rump. Nor are there any protuberances on the muscles. The stature is rather long than tall. The trunk is vaulted, and the bones are strong, and the leanness of the horses is striking. But one forgets the ugly appearance of these horses as this is set off by their fine qualities: their sober nature, cleverness and their ability to endure any injuries very well. (Vegetius *Mul.* 3.6.5)

True, these horses were of a hardy though ugly breed, but what must be remembered is that here Vegetius, like Ammianus, is subconsciously comparing the pasture-fed horse of the Huns with the stall-fed horse of the Romans. In general the Hun horse was far better at climbing, jumping and swimming than the Roman horse, and the main equine characteristics looked for were a flat back for ease of riding and the long neck of a good jumper.

Curiously, however, Orosius (7.34) says that in the time of Theodosius I, the Huns had acquired Roman horses. These relatively big animals, accustomed to grain, would have found it extremely tough to adapt to, and survive on, a diet of grass and bark. Perhaps the

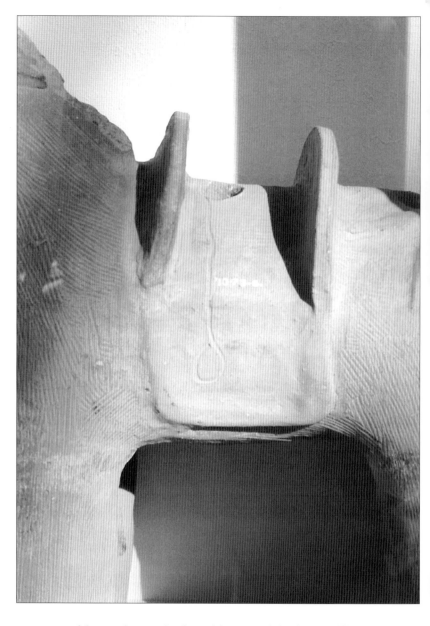

Hanswa horse (Edinburgh, Royal Museum, 10.73–6) from Osato district, Saitama Province, Japan. It carries the universal wood-frame saddle of the Asiatic horse-archer, with its high front and back arches. The Huns used one of a similar design, usually of birch wood. (Author's collection)

answer to this puzzle may be found in one of the later military treatises of Leo VI (r. AD 886–912). In his *Problemata* (7.9.48, cf. Mauricius *Strategikon* 7.1.12), Leo, drawing upon the accumulated experiences of the 5th and 6th centuries, puts his information in the form of question and answer:

Q. What must the general do, if the nation [of the enemy] be Scythian or Hun?

A. He should attack them about the month of February or March, when their horses are weakened by the hardships of winter.

In other words, by the late winter pasture-fed horses could do less work than the stall-fed horses, which had their hay and grain brought

to them. To overcome this seasonal disadvantage, Roman remounts notwithstanding, the Huns made a practice of travelling with a number of reserve mounts to ensure that they always had a fresh one when needed (Ammianus 17.12.3, cf. Mauricius *Strategikon* 11.2.9–14). Every horse belonging to a particular rider had to resemble as closely as possible the others in his string. In the grave of a Hun warrior discovered in Hungary were found the skeletons of two horses, and their sizes were in all respects almost identical. Obviously, on the owner's death his choice animals were not ridden again. As was the custom with pastoral societies, a rider set a high value on his horses and thus was extremely reluctant to let a stranger ride one.

Although the Hun empire was not a pastoral nomad society in the 5th century, it does not mean that horses did not play a major role in Hun society – their skills on horseback seem to have been preserved and many of them were fine horse-warriors who could handle their horses expertly and ride for many hours without fatigue.

Stirrups and saddles

The excellent horsemanship of the Huns has often been ascribed to their use of stirrups. Stirrups are usually seen in terms of how they could help the horseman be more effective, either as a horse-archer or when

Carolingian horsemen in the St-Gallen Psalter. The riders use rigid-tree saddles, along with pear-shaped stirrups and prick spurs. They wear long mail shirts and open-faced helmets, and carry lances. It would appear that this particular unit was equipped for 'shock troop' engagements. (Esther Carré)

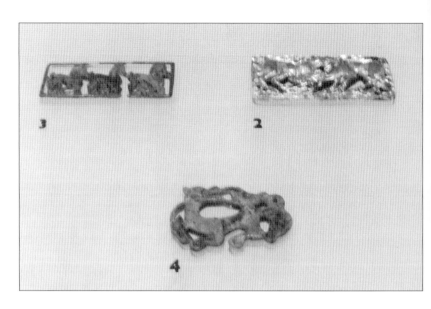

Three harness ornaments of bronze, decorated with various animals such as ibex and deer (Edinburgh, Royal Museum, A.1963.502, A.1966.347, A.1978.613), Han dynasty (206 BC–AD 220). Small portable pieces such as these clearly show the influence of the decorative art of central Asian nomads. (Esther Carré)

using other weapons. What is often overlooked is the fact that stirrups also gave support to the legs on long-distance rides and reduced the effects of the cold by improving the circulation in the rider's legs. This was, in truth, probably why they were developed in one of the coldest horse-rearing parts of the world. However, no such devices have been found that are attributed to the Huns, and the importance of this development has been over-emphasized by many historians, particularly in the military context. For the Huns, it was their innate skill and small mounts that gave them an advantage over most western horsemen, not the stirrup.

Stirrups first appear in the 2nd and 1st centuries BC in Indian (toe stirrups) and Scythian (hook stirrups) contexts. Toe stirrups were simple loops that held the big toe, and thus their use was somewhat limited by climate and footwear. The true, fully developed rigid wood- or metal-framed stirrup designed to take the whole foot is mentioned for the first time in a Chinese chronicle of AD 477, and is seen in votive ceramics of the Northern Wei dynasty (AD 386–534), and again at the time of the Tang dynasty (AD 618–907). The chronicle, a biography of a military magnate, reports that the stirrup was brought to China by the Juan-Juan. It was the Avar descendants of these steppe-dwellers who were to bring metal-framed stirrups to Europe.

The rigid stirrup was also present in Korea by the early 6th century, as shown by a horse-archer riding with stirrups in a fresco from the tomb of Buyô-Zuka at Tong K'ou, North Korea. The iron pear-shaped form, the ancestor of medieval European types, appears in Japan around AD 470–550, and is first in Europe in 7th-century Avar graves in Hungary. The Avars were ethnically related to the Huns and had settled in Europe in AD 564. In the west, the stirrup first appears in Beatus' *Commentary on the Apocalypse* (*c.* AD 776), showing the Four Horsemen of the Apocalypse. The St-Gallen Psalter (*c.* AD 863) depicts Carolingian horsemen using stirrups, although the archaeological and literary evidence suggests that the stirrup was little appreciated and little used by the Carolingians during the 8th and 9th centuries, being established only by the following century.

Horse harness pendant and eight mounts of sliver-gilt and silver inlays of carnelian and glass (London, British Museum, MME.1923.7–16, 16–23, 27–28) from Kerch, Crimea. Dated to the 4th century, the craftsmanship is Roman in origin, and probably decorated the harness of either a Goth or Hun horse. (Esther Carré)

The riding equipment of the Huns was rudimentary. As well as lack of stirrups, they did not use spurs, but urged their horses on with riding whips. Equally, the frame saddle used by the Huns (and later the Avars) was more suitable for a horse-archer than the four-horned saddle used by the Romans. It was also more comfortable to ride and much less wearing to a horse. Attila, preparing for a hero's death by immolation after the battle of Châlons, had ordered a funeral pyre of saddles. Though the Avars are credited with first introducing the frame saddle to Europe, here we have an indication that the Huns also possessed such saddles, in the Avar style. A frame saddle consisted of a wooden frame with leather cushioning lying either side, a type found as far afield in time and space as Xïongnú graves at Noin Ula (Rudenko 1969) and Scythian graves at Pazyryk (Rudenko 1970: 129–37). In a European context, the wood-frame saddle had a straight vertical arch in front and a larger arch behind (Maenchen-Helfen 1973: 208–10).

These mule saddles allow us to understand better the makeup of that used by the Huns. A wooden, lateral frame supports vertical arches, front and back, the seat between being padded with leather. Additional padding beneath the frame protects the spine of the mount. (Author's collection)

In western military philosophy the primary function of the saddle is seen as a means to provide the rider with a secure and comfortable seat in 'shock troop' engagements. Lack of a retaining and firmly constructed saddle reduced the power that a rider could harness so as to deliver maximum poundage to a thrusting lance. Too violent a movement would detach both weapon and rider from the horse's back.

To achieve this condition, a rigid saddle is necessary. Consisting of a wooden frame (tree) with padding, it permits the rider to employ greater force in weapon thrusts without the added danger of being easily knocked off his horse. A rigid-tree saddle, along with pear-shaped stirrups and prick spurs, would eventually make it possible to control the horse with thigh, knee and ankle, and allow an expert horseman to fight effectively with a lance. The lateral stability provided by the stirrup was real and injected a vital and previously missing element into shock cavalry. In tandem with the longitudinal support of a rigid-tree saddle, the stirrup welded rider and horse together sufficiently well to open up an entirely new means of attack. Rather than thrusting out himself, the lancer could now hold his weapon at rest in the crook of his arm, using the combined weight of his body and his charging mount to deliver a blow of unprecedented violence. This arrangement had the additional benefit of freeing the opposite arm to control the reins and carry the kite-shaped shield that was the rider's major means of turning aside equivalent blows. Balance between offence and defence was also essential to the stability of the system.

In the words of Leo the Deacon (*fl.* AD 950), 'a general who has a force of 5,000 to 6,000 seasoned cavalrymen under him needs, with the help of God, no more troops' (*Historiaum* 10. 230). By taking its cue from the east, the emperors made shock cavalry the heart of the Byzantine army. The cavalrymen of Leo VI (*Tactica* 12.806–43) wore a steel helmet, a thigh-length hooded mail coat (*zaba*), gauntlets and steel shoes. The horses of officers and of front-rank troopers were furnished with steel frontlets and poitrails, but all horsemen had rigid-saddles, iron stirrups and prick spurs. The trooper's weapons included a

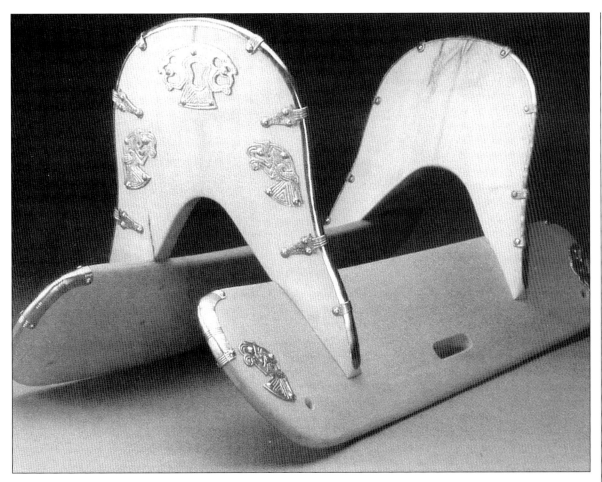

Reconstruction of the wood-
frame saddle (Mannheim, Reiss
Museum) from grave 446, Wesel-
Bilich. This is decorated with
eagle appliqués. It is high in the
back and front, thus providing
a secure seat for a horse-archer
to discharge his arrows in any
direction. (Esther Carré)

broadsword, a dagger, a bow and bow-case, covered quiver for 30–40 arrows and a lance of Avar type.

Yet Byzantine cavalry, like their eastern opponents, still relied on the composite bow as their primary weapon. In the west, however, this was not the case. Writing a little more than a century after Leo the Deacon, the astonished Anna Komnena reckoned that 'the first charge of the Frankish cavalry was irresistible', the Latin knight having the impetus to 'bore his way through the walls of Babylon' (*Alexiad* 5.4, 13.8). Astonishing, perhaps, but Leo VI had already advised the following: 'So formidable is the charge of the Frankish chivalry with their broadsword, lance, and shield, that it is best to avoid a pitched battle with them until you have put all the chances on your own side' (*Tactica* 18.966–67).

ON CAMPAIGN

It was herd management as much as fighting skills that made the Huns so adept at confronting sedentary agriculturalists. These horse-warriors, the chroniclers say, did not commit themselves irrevocably to attack. Instead they approached the enemy in a loose crescent formation, which threatened less mobile opponents with encirclement around the flanks. If strongly resisted at any point, they would stage a withdrawal, the object of which was to draw the enemy out of its chosen position and into an ill-judged pursuit. They engaged in close combat only when things were clearly going in their favour. To achieve this, they harried and intimidated the enemy with volleys of arrows shot at long range.

Low-level operations

To obtain what they needed to ease and enliven nomadic life it was not uncommon for steppe-dwellers to go raiding instead of trading. A Han chronicler says of the Xiongnú: 'In good times they are accustomed to following their cattle, enjoying field sports and getting drunk; in bad times everyone prepares for war in order to make raids' (Bichurin 1950: 1.40).

Hun raiders, much like the predatory Xiongnú, would strike fast and hard, only to disappear in an instant. From China to Europe, sedentary cultures around the steppe-rim had always been at risk of sudden attack by these centaur-like people, able to shoot with extraordinary accuracy and power while at full gallop.

> The Xiongnú move on the feet of swift horses, and in their breasts beat the hearts of beasts. They shift from place to place as swiftly as a flock of birds; so that it is extremely difficult to corner them and bring them under control … it would not be expedient to attack the Xiongnú. Better to make peace with them. (quoted in Greer 1975: 24)

So advised Han An-kuo, in his capacity as minister to the Han emperor Ching (r. 156–41 BC). Likewise, the Huns inspired terror by the speed of their movements. With two or three horses each, a Hun war party unencumbered by wagons could cover some 160 kilometres a day over favourable terrain. Thus, with their system of reserve mounts, they

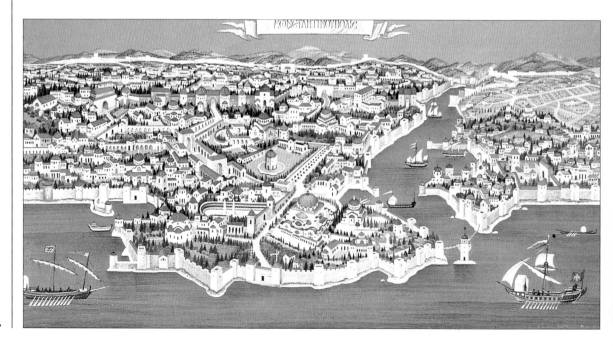

Greek postcard depicting Constantinople and its impregnable defences. No enemy ever breached this barrier until Mehmet II took the city in 1453 using the latest technology – gunpowder weapons. Attila, a thousand years before, was granted a chance to do so when an earthquake reduced the walls to rubble. (Author's collection)

could ensure that no messenger travelled faster than they did. As a result the first the occupants of a settlement learned of the arrival of a hostile band of Huns was probably a cloud of dust, followed by the dull thud of hooves, then by a rain of arrows.

High-level operations

Raiders hoped to gain as much plunder as possible and then retire without undue fuss. The plunder taken by raiders tended to be confined to easily movable items, and most raids did not penetrate very deep into Roman territory. In contrast large-scale military activity depended upon effective leadership. The Huns mounted major attacks against the eastern empire in AD 441, 443 and 447, and in AD 451 and 452 they attacked the western empire. However, these high-level operations were only feasible because of the unification of the various Danubian tribes, both and Hun and non-Hun alike, under a single leader, Attila.

Clashes between the Hun empire and the Romans allowed for some prior preparation and planning, mainly because of Attila's autocratic position. In AD 451, for instance, he made the deliberate decision to attack the western rather than the eastern empire since, 'it seemed best for him first to undertake the greater war and march against the west' (Priscus fr. 20.1). Before Attila, the Huns were not strong enough seriously to threaten either half of the empire, and after his death the Balkan provinces did not suffer from a major attack (as opposed to raiding) until the Onogur Huns ravaged the area in AD 502. Because of their raids deep into imperial territory, Anastasius I (r. AD 491–518) built the Long Walls across the Thracian peninsula, which ran some 56 kilometres west of Constantinople from Selymbria on the Marmara to the Black Sea, in order to protect the hinterland of the capital.

Battle

Steppe-dwellers preferred to fight in a loose formation, continually harassing their quarry with deadly barrages of missiles and avoiding hand-to-hand combat, which made them difficult opponents to handle on the battlefield. They would also take every opportunity to enhance their terrifying image, and, in particular, Ammianus (31.2.8) writes of the Huns as attacking with much disorderly movement while making savage noises. Not surprisingly, they quickly gained a fearsome reputation and became known in battle for the ferocity of their mounted charges, their unexpected retreats, their superb horsemanship and their skill with bow and arrow.

The best account of Hun horsemanship in battle is undoubtedly provided by Ammianus (31.2.8–9, cf. Mauricius *Strategikon* 11.2.15–31). The Huns of his day occasionally fought as individuals but more usually entered the fray in tactical formation. Being lightly equipped allowed them to move swiftly and unexpectedly. One tactic especially perplexed the Romans: the Huns would purposely and suddenly divide into scattered bands and would rush about in 'disorder' here and there, and as a result initiate considerable slaughter. First they fought from a distance using missile fire, maintaining an incessant barrage until the enemy was sufficiently weakened or demoralized. Then they galloped over the intervening space and engaged in hand-to-hand fighting.

A Hun charge was executed with such speed and suddenness that it usually overwhelmed everyone and everything in its path.

Battle of Châlons (20 June AD 451)

Aëtius' coalition of Romans, Visigoths and Alans fought Attila's equally diverse army of Huns, Ostrogoths and Gepids to a standstill on the chalky grasslands somewhere in what is now Champagne, northern France. Some believe the site closer to Troyes (Tricassis), at Méry-sur-Seine (Mauriacum), possibly near the village of Châtres (originally *castra*, a camp), than to Châlons-sur-Marne (Duro-Catalaunum). If this is correct, the battle – known sometimes by the name of Locus Mauriacus and sometimes by that of the Catalaunian Plains – is most likely to have taken place on the broad, flat plain between Méry and Estissac.

In Fritz Lang's two-part epic *Die Nibelungen* (1924), Attila appears as the very essence of evil. This is Part II, *La Vengeance de Kriemhilde*, with Rudolf Klein-Rogge as a fearsome, albeit cursed, Attila. (Esther Carré)

Having secured the Rhine, Attila swept into central Gaul and invested Aureliani (Orléans-sur-Loire). Had he gained his objective, he would have been in a strong position to subdue the Visigoths in Aquitania Secunda, but Aëtius put together a formidable coalition for the defence of Gaul. Traditionally foes of the Romans, the Visigoths and Alans were nonetheless wedded to Aëtius' cause through a common hatred (and fear) of the Huns.

Attila for his part, however, did not lack friends. Gaiseric, king of the Vandals, had already played a role in the prelude to the battle. He had urged Attila to attack the Visigoths because of the enmity between Vandal and Visigoth. A generation earlier Gaiseric's son had married the daughter of Theodoric I, king of the Visigoths, but in AD 442 Valentinianus III agreed to the betrothal of his daughter to Gaiseric's son. The Visigoth princess was returned to her people, her nose and ears inhumanly mutilated (Priscus fr. 20.2, Jordanes 36.184). When Attila crossed the Rhine, the Visigoths joined Aëtius, but the Vandals stayed out of the war.

Attila had not expected such vigorous action on the part of the Romans, and he was too wise to allow his army to be trapped outside the walls of Aureliani, so he raised the siege (14 June). Withdrawing, Attila made for open grasslands to the north where he could use his horse-warriors to best advantage.

The Huns of Attila, by the Spanish artist Ulpiano Checa y Sanz (1860–1916). Attila (right, foreground), at the head of his horse-warriors, sweeps into Italy. In western psyche the Huns remain the dark menace to civilization, a stereotype first articulated by the Graeco-Roman chroniclers. (Ancient Art and Architecture)

The imperial army deployed with the Romans on the left flank and the Visigoths, under the aged Theodoric, on the right. The Alans occupied the centre under Sangiban, a king whose loyalty to any cause but his own preservation was considered highly doubtful by Aëtius (Jordanes 37.196, cf. 194). On the right wing of the Hun army Attila stationed the bulk of his Germanic allies. The Ostrogoths, under their king Valamer, took the left, opposite the Visigoths, and in the centre Attila placed the best of his troops, the Huns.

The battlefield itself was a large level area of '100 *leuva* in length … and 70 in width' (*c.* 300 acres, Jordanes 36.192) rising by a sharp slope to a ridge, and cut by a stream. Precise details of the battle are lacking, the only account being that of Jordanes. Theodoric apparently despatched his son Thorismond to occupy the high ground overlooking the left flank of the Huns. Attila responded by detaching some troops to drive away Thorismond, but these, in their effort to gain the top of the ridge, were easily routed. Attila, casting aside the usual Hun tactic of first softening up the opposition with missile fire, then launched the rest of his forces straight at the imperial army. In an allegorical speech to his men, Attila is supposed to have said the following: 'The Romans are poor soldiers, keeping together in rank and file. They are contemptible, the only worthy enemies are the Alans and the Visigoths' (Jordanes 39.204). Despite the wavering Alans scattering on the Huns' initial charge, the battle was hard fought, lasting for most of the day, with heavy casualties on both sides.

Theodoric was amongst the slain, trampled to death by his own Visigoths or (as some said) slain by the spear of Andag, an Ostrogoth, but nightfall saw the imperial army in possession of the field. Attila had pulled back his exhausted and battered forces into his wagon laager, thus preparing for a fight to the death on the following day. Tradition has it that Attila, determined not be taken alive, piled saddles within his wagons to form a pyre upon which he would fling himself. But Aëtius, fearing his allies, the Visigoths, scarcely less than the Huns, forbore from destroying a possible counterpoise to their power. He let Attila off the hook and allowed the Huns to withdraw unmolested (Thompson 1948: 142–43).

Ironically this battle has been reckoned as one of the most decisive in world history, the battle that saved western Europe from Attila. Yet considering its violence, it decided very little. Both sides sustained immense losses and neither was victorious. Keeping his multi-tribal army intact, Attila retreated to his wooden capital in Pannonia and the next year launched a major offensive into Italy.

GLOSSARY

bucellarii	'Biscuit-eaters' – armed retainers of Roman/Byzantine commander
bucellatum	'Hardtack' – double-baked campaign bread
comes/comites	'Companion' – translated as count, commander of a field force
comes domesticorum	Commander of the *domestici* protecting the emperor
dux/duces	'Leader' – translated as duke, commander of sector of frontier
foederati	Barbarians, under their ethnic leaders, serving Roman/Byzantine emperor
kvasses	Fermented mare's milk
Lames/lamellae	Narrow vertical plate
Leuva	Gallic distance approximating to 1,500 Roman paces
magister equitum	Master of Cavalry – title given to senior Roman commander
magister militum	Master of Soldiers – collective title for both services
magister peditum	Master of Infantry – title given to senior Roman commander
pteruges	'Feathers' – leather fringing on armour
scholae palatinae	Household troops protecting the Roman/Byzantine emperor
solidus/solidi	Late-Roman gold coin (4.54 grams = five-sixths weight of old *aureus*)
spangenhelm	Conical segmented helmet of Danubian origin

BIBLIOGRAPHY

Bichurin, N.Y., *Collected References to Peoples Inhabiting Central Asia in Antiquity*, vol. 1, Moscow–Leningrad (1950)

Elton, H., *Warfare in Roman Europe, AD 350–425*, Clarendon Press, Oxford (1996, reprinted 1997)

Gordon, C.D., *The Age of Attila*, University of Michigan Press, Ann Arbor (1960, reprinted 1966)

Greer, J.P., *The Armies and Enemies of Ancient China*, Wargames Research Group, Worthing (1975)

Hodgkin, T., *Huns, Vandals, and the Fall of the Roman Empire*, Stackpole Books, Mechanicsburg, PA (1996)

Howarth, P., *Attila, King of the Huns: The Man and the Myth*, Constable, London (1994, reprinted 1997)

Karasulas, A., *Mounted Archers of the Steppe, 600 BC–AD 1300* (Elite 120), Osprey, Oxford (2004)

Kassai, L., *Horseback Archery*, Püski Kiadó, Budapest (2002)

Laing, J., *Warriors of the Dark Age*, Sutton, Stroud (2000)

Liebeschuetz, J.H.W.G., *Barbarians and Bishops*, Clarendon Press, Oxford (1991)

Lindner, R.P., 'Nomadism, Horses and Huns', *Past and Present* 92 (1981), pp.1–19

McEwen, E., 'Nomadic archery: some observations on composite bow design and construction', in P. Denwood (ed), *Arts of the Eurasian Steppelands*, School of Oriental and African Studies, London (1978), pp.188–202

McLeod, W., 'The range of the ancient bow', *Phoenix* 19 (1965), pp.1–14

Maenchen-Helfen, O.J., 'Huns and Hsiung-nu', *Byzantion* 17 (1945), pp.222–43

– *The World of the Huns*, University of California Press, Berkeley (1973)

Man, J., *Attila: The Barbarian King who Challenged Rome*, Bantam Press, London (2005)

Massey, D., 'Roman archery tested', *Military Illustrated* 74 (1994), pp.36–39

Mommsen, T., 'Aëtius', *Hermes* 36 (1901), pp.516–47

Moss, J.R., 'The effects of the policies of Aëtius on the history of western Europe', *Historia* 72 (1973), pp.711–31

Nicolle, D., *Attila and the Nomad Hordes* (Elite 30), Osprey, Oxford (1990)

Rudenko, S.I. (trans. H. Pollems), *Die Kultur der Hsiung-Nu und die Hügelgräber von Noin Ula*, Rudolf Habelt, Bonn (1969)

– (trans. M.W. Thompson), *Frozen Tombs of Siberia: The Pazyryk Burials of Iron Age Horsemen*, J.M. Dent & Sons, London (1970)

Selby, S., *Chinese Archery*, Hong Kong University Press, Hong Kong (2000, reprinted 2003)

Täeckholm, U., 'Aëtius and the battle on the Catalaunian Fields', *Opuscula Romana* 7 (1969), pp.259–76

Thompson, E.A., *A History of Attila and the Huns*, Clarendon Press, Oxford (1948)

Vainshtein, S., (trans M. Colenso), *Nomads of South Siberia: The Pastoral Economies of Tuva*, Cambridge Studies in Social Anthropology 25, Cambridge University Press, Cambridge (1980)

Wess, R., *Victory Secrets of Attila, the Hun*, Doubleday, New York (1993)

COLOUR PLATE COMMENTARY

A: THE HORSE WARRIOR

The key to survival on the central Asian steppe was the horse (1), invaluable for transport, herding, hunting and warfare. Skeletal remains of steppe horses found in Hun burials reveal their small, tough, stocky build and short, broad muzzle. The animals were marked either by branding, or by cutting the ears. It would appear that they were gelded. Despite what Vegetius (*Mul*. 3.6.5) says, the mane of a riding-horse was probably trimmed. Wind blowing through an untrimmed mane would have impeded the rider when shooting his bow.

As there were no stirrups the rider had to grip the horse with his knees. To prevent him slipping, the front and back of the wood-frame saddle were stiffened and bridged by vertical arches. Plaques (2) decorated with repoussé feather patterns are characteristic of Hun burials, and these were probably attached to saddlebows.

The saddle (3) could be secured by three girths – front, middle and rear – though often only the front and rear saddle-

girths were employed. The front one was tightly secured to the saddle-frame and the rear one was lashed over the frame. The breast-strap and crupper were normally only used on long journeys, when they would be fastened to the saddle-frame by means of leather loops. Harnessing straps could be decorated with various pendants (4). Contemporary Graeco-Roman writers took every opportunity to boost the Huns' terrifying image in the eyes of their readers, describing them eating, sleeping and even performing bodily functions on horseback. To be a Hun male was to be a Hun warrior, and the great majority of them were primarily horse-archers. However, they differed from most others in that they were also prepared to fight at close quarters.

In appearance a species of centaur, half-horse, half-man, with scarred cheeks, broad faces and flat noses, weather-beaten complexions, and shaggy, with hair and animal skins, the Huns were undoubtedly terrifying in combat. This warrior (5) rides the ill-shaped but hardy steppe breed of horse. He is dressed in woollen tunic and breeches, while his jacket, leggings and cap are of goatskin. His calf-length leather boots are heel-less. His weapons are the composite bow and bone-pointed arrows, small shield and light spear.

A common tool of the herder, the lasso is also used to bring down an enemy horseman or capture someone on foot. Lassos are made of soft, well-processed leather, and the rider would carry it coiled up and strapped to the rear arch of the saddle, as shown here, or else slung over his

**Kurt Rydle in the role of Verdi's *Attila*,
Théâtre du Chatelet, Paris (1982). On its première
(17 March 1846), Verdi was in trouble with the
ruling Austrian authorities. When Ezio offers Attila
the rest of the world provided he himself can
retain Italy, the political implications are obvious.
(Esther Carré)**

Silver-gilt amphora of Greek craftsmanship, 4th century BC, from the Chertomlyk Kurgan, Ukraine. A Scythian warrior hobbles his horse, a typical example of the hardy steppe breed. Its mane has been trimmed so as not to impede the rider when firing his bow. (Author's collection)

shoulder. In addition a rider would normally carry a whip, with a wooden handle and a fairly thick thong of rawhide serving as a lash. The whip handle would be pasted over with fine leather, while on its lower end is a leather loop.

B: ARMS AND EQUIPMENT

The composite bow (1) is a complex union of horn, wood and sinew. The core is wood with a heavy layer of horn bonded on to the belly and several cables of stretched sinew on the back. The belly is the side nearest the archer when the bow is drawn, the back that side away from the archer and facing the target. The tips, where the bowstring is notched, are reinforced with bone or horn ear-laths (2). When strung, the bow is opened back against its natural curve and held that way by the bowstring. More powerful than the later longbow, it can penetrate armour at 100 metres. When not in use the bow, still strung, is housed in a case (3) carried by the front of the left thigh.

A man fashioned his own arrows, their length equalling the length of his arm to the fingertips. They are kept in an hourglass quiver with a closing flap (4). The shape allows the accommodation of arrows with barbs up for easier arrowhead selection. While socketed arrowheads penetrate more effectively, tanged arrowheads are less likely to break.

Additionally they are easier to range, thus enabling more rapid shooting.

The most effective method for shooting on horseback is the Mongolian style, which employs the thumb only. This requires the use of a bone or ivory thumb-ring (5), slipped over the thumb of the draw-hand, with the bowstring lying in the slight depression seen here at the top of the ring. The forefinger clenches the thumb inwards, and when the archer nocks the arrow and pulls the bowstring, the ring slides gradually forward to arrive at the fold of the thumb joint. The thumb-draw is fast, thus allowing a greater speed of delivery.

Despite their fame as horse-archers, the Huns are also known for their long double-edged swords (6). The sword is hung from a loose sword-belt, which rests on the hips (7). The hip-belt derives from a Sassanid type in which the belt runs through an elongated scabbard-slide on the outer face of the weapon's scabbard. This system suits the mounted warrior but makes the weapon difficult to draw when on foot. European Huns also carry a long dagger, which is hung horizontally across the abdomen.

C: RAIDING

For the Huns raiding was not only a necessity during times of hardship but became a well-ingrained habit, for as they became more skilled at raiding they increasingly gave up any attempt at supplementing their subsistence in other ways. Physically tough and logistically mobile, they had the power to rob and, while they remained essentially herders, this inclination led to a permanent state of raiding. The Romans frequently bought them off, which was not difficult to do, as they raided principally for plunder. Without a doubt the Huns, who were quick to take advantage, saw this approach as a sign of imperial weakness: during the decade AD 440–50 the eastern empire paid 13,000 pounds of gold to buy peace.

Relying on no more than the composite bow and a string of horses, raiding parties were small, lightly loaded and fast moving. Having penetrated the frontier they usually remained dispersed, but often concentrated if a Roman army entered the area. Nevertheless, raids were not intended to be bloody affairs but a means of acquiring plunder by stealth. The return journey was made as rapidly as possible, despite the acquisition of booty, and by travelling without rest or sleep the raiders usually made a successful escape. They avoided fighting.

D: THE PARTHIAN SHOT

With their highly developed tactic of rapid-fire barrage shooting, the usual opening manoeuvre was for the Huns to wear down the enemy from a distance. Thus successive bands of horsemen would advance, wheel and retreat, shooting volleys of arrows as they did so. The latter would be done at high elevation, a skill developed by steppe-dwellers, which meant that arrows would land almost vertically on a target. Each successive band would relieve the one before to keep up an incessant barrage. This skirmishing would continue until the enemy was sufficiently weakened or demoralized.

The Huns' favourite – and winning – battlefield tactic was to outflank, harass and even encircle the foe; here their

strengths of speed, mobility and firepower were exploited to the full. Riding at full gallop and parallel with the enemy, the archer turns in his saddle and fires sideways – the arrow flying almost flat – reloads, fires again, and again. The archer's technique here would be to release his shot when the horse is in full flight. So as to fire one arrow after another at speed, he might hold a bunch of arrows in his left hand against the bow.

Of course not all opponents were static. For a more mobile enemy, the Huns had other tactics. In particular there was the feigned retreat, which would, with luck, draw the opposition forward far enough to tackle them piecemeal. As the archer gallops directly away from the enemy, he still engages him by using the technique of the backward 'Parthian shot'.

E: BATTLE OF CHÂLONS

When the fighting started it was a straightforward pounding-match, with no elaborate tactics. Victory would go to the side that stood and did not flinch. With the battle lines so extended there was little opportunity for the Huns to try their preferred encircling trick. Attila thus concentrated his main attack, using his best troops, the Huns, in the centre. Here Aëtius had stationed the reputedly unreliable Sangiban and his Alans, where they had no choice but to stand fast and fight.

This scene shows Sangiban, in the third rank of the Alans, watching the Hun van as it sweeps down. The Huns, controlling their charging mounts with thigh and knee, are fitting arrows to the strings of their bows. The Alan king knows that as long as his warriors keep formation, protected by their shields, the mounted foe will not press home a charge against an array of spear-points. It is not to be.

F: SPOILS OF WAR

Spoils were a vital source of income. Money, precious metals, horses, cattle, other movable property, arms, armour and hostages formed the basic booty for the Hun, and their conflicts with the Romans were for the most part a series of large-scale raids intended to gain plunder. Outright set-piece battles with imperial forces were rare – the battle of Châlons being a notable exception.

Gold, silver and jewellery were naturally preferred, although they would rarely be available in large amounts unless towns were sacked. Food or drink was also plundered, and often consumed on the spot. This could be dangerous, as sated raiders could be caught by surprise. Nevertheless, under Attila's effective leadership low-intensity raids could be turned into major invasions, and this scene shows the aftermath of a full-scale engagement. The victorious Huns are busy scouring the battlefield for loot, rounding up stray horses and collecting prisoners. Some of them are equipping themselves with Roman arms stripped from the dead.

Egg-tempera on wood icon, 18th century, Athens. The image shows the siege of Constantinople by the Avars in AD 626. Like the Huns, the Turkic Avars, who are depicted here as Ottoman Turks, were Central Asian horse-warriors and shared the Huns' grand ambitions and ruthless drive. (Author's collection)

INDEX